# GENERAL ENGLISH GRAMMAR

(Useful for School, College and Competitive Exams.)

*By*
**J.V. Subrahmanyam**

**FIRST EDITION**
An imprint of Sura Books (Pvt) Ltd.
(An ISO 9001:2000 Certified Company)
Chennai ● Ernakulam
Bengalooru ● Thiruvananthapuram

**Price: ₹40.00**

©PUBLISHERS

# General English Grammar

### By
### J.V. Subrahmanyam

| | | |
|---|---|---|
| This Edition | : | March, 2011 |
| Size | : | 1/8 Demy |
| Pages | : | 144 |
| Code No. | : | G 34 |

## Price: ₹40.00

ISBN: 81-7478-148-X

[NO ONE IS PERMITTED TO COPY OR TRANSLATE IN ANY OTHER LANGUAGE THE CONTENTS OF THIS BOOK OR PART THEREOF IN ANY FORM WITHOUT THE WRITTEN PERMISSION OF THE PUBLISHERS]

### FIRST EDITION
[An imprint of Sura Books (Pvt) Ltd.]

**Head Office:** 1620, 'J' Block, 16th Main Road, Anna Nagar, Chennai - 600 040. Phones: 044-26162173, 26161099.

**Branches :**
- XXXII/2328, New Kalavath Road, Opp. to BSNL, Near Chennoth Glass, Palarivattom, Ernakulam - 682 025. Phones: 0484-3205797, 2535636.
- TC 27/2162, Chirakulam Road, Statue, Thiruvananthapuram - 695 001.
- 3638/A, IVth Cross, Opp. to Malleswaram Railway Station, Gayathri Nagar, Back gate of Subramaniya Nagar, Bengalooru - 560 021. Phone: 080-23324950.

Printed at G.T. Krishna Press, Chennai - 600 102 and Published by V.V.K.Subburaj for First Edition [An imprint of Sura Books (Pvt) Ltd.] 1620, 'J' Block, 16th Main Road, Anna Nagar, Chennai - 600 040. Phones: 26162173, 26161099. Fax: (91) 44-26162173. e-mail: enquiry@surabooks.com; website: www.surabooks.com

# CONTENTS

| | | Pages |
|---|---|---|
| 1. | Parts of Speech | 1 |
| 2. | Nouns | 4 |
| 3. | Gender | 9 |
| 4. | Number | 12 |
| 5. | Forming Possessives | 15 |
| 6. | Adjectives | 18 |
| 7. | Degrees of Comparison | 23 |
| 8. | Determiners | 26 |
| 9. | Articles | 27 |
| 10. | Pronouns | 36 |
| 11. | Verbs | 43 |
| 12. | Regular and Irregular Verbs | 49 |
| 13. | Modal Auxiliaries | 54 |
| 14. | Question Tags | 59 |
| 15. | Adverbs | 60 |
| 16. | Prepositions | 64 |
| 17. | Conjunctions | 69 |
| 18. | Interjections | 72 |
| 19. | Sentences | 72 |
| 20. | Subject and Predicate | 73 |
| 21. | Tense | 81 |
| 22. | Active and Passive Voice | 93 |

| | | Pages |
|---|---|---|
| 23. | Direct and Indirect Speech | 101 |
| 24. | Simple Compound, Complex and Compound Complex | 106 |
| 25. | Non-finites | 113 |
| 26. | The Participle | 116 |
| 27. | Gerund | 118 |
| 28. | Prefixes and Suffixes | 119 |
| 29. | Synonyms | 123 |
| 30. | Antonyms | 124 |
| 31. | One-word Substitutes | 127 |
| 32. | Similes | 129 |
| 33. | Idioms | 130 |
| 34. | Word Doubles | 131 |
| 35. | Test | 133 |

# GENERAL ENGLISH GRAMMAR

Every word in a sentence has a function. According to the work they do in a sentence, words are divided into different categories called **Parts of speech.** They are 8 in number. One piece of information a dictionary provides about a word is its part of speech. For example, if you look up the word "flipper" in a dictionary you will find out not only how to spell it and what it means (limb of turtle, penguin, etc used in swimming) but also what part of speech it is - a noun.

## Parts of Speech

1. Noun
2. Adjective
3. Pronoun
4. Verb
5. Adverb
6. Preposition
7. Conjunction
8. Interjection

## 1. Noun :

Nouns are the names of people, places, things, ideas, actions or qualities. **Examples :** Renuka, Gita, Shyam, Beasant Nagar, Paris, Italy, Oil, Memory, Card.

## 2. Adjective :

Adjectives describe (qualify) nouns and pronouns. 'House' is a noun that names a kind of structure, but to indicate a specific house, you may want to describe it further by calling it a "spacious, white house". **Spacious** and **white** are adjectives.

**Examples : Green** chair, **Melodious** song, **Tall** boy, **Skilful** surgeon.

## 3. Pronoun :

Pronouns replace nouns. In the sentence, "Vimala entered the room but she did not speak to me," the word "she" a pronoun refers to Vimala. **Examples :** I, you, he, his, she, hers, theirs, us, we etc.,

## 4. Verb :

Verbs refer to actions or states. **Examples :** laugh, talk, jump, fight.

## 5. Adverb :

Adverbs modify verbs, adjectives and other adverbs. They tell you when, where, or how something happens. **Examples :** to describe more vividly, the fact "The baby slept" you might say, "The baby slept **soundly.**" 'Soundly' describes how the baby slept. So it is an adverb. Very, tomorrow, loudly, brightly etc. are adverbs.

## 6. Preposition :

Prepositions connect nouns, pronouns and noun phrases to other words in a sentence and indicate their relationships. Prepositions are placed before a noun or a pronoun. **Example :** The cat sat **on** the wall. In this sentence, the preposition **on** connects the noun 'Cat' to the noun phrase 'the wall' and indicates the position of the cat in relation to the wall. **Examples :** After, before, by, of, with etc,.

## 7. Conjunction :

Conjunctions connect words, phrases, clauses and sentences. **Examples:** bread **and** butter, so near **yet** so far, the journey was tough **because** the road was terribly bad. Ram is good **but** Peter is bad. Unless, since, if, or, while etc. are conjunctions.

## 8. Interjection :

Interjections express emotions, and feelings. They are common in informal writing. **Examples :** Hurrah!, Alas!, Great!, Aha!, Wow!, Ouch!, Che!.

## 9. Articles :

Many Grammarians include 'Articles' in Adjectives. Wherever they are, 'a', 'an' and 'the' are the articles.

# Exercise 1

## Directions :

Identify the words printed boldly in the given sentences and write the correct part of speech on the line.

Example :

Ouch : Interjection        **Ouch** ! I have stubbed my toe.

1. _____ Asoka was a **wise** king.
2. _____ The cow **jumped** over the moon.
3. _____ Old pillows can be made new **easily**.
4. _____ She took out a gun **from** her bag.
5. _____ I am going to give **my** Barbie dolls away.
6. _____ She wants to sell all her **household** goods **and** go to Timbuctoo.
7. _____ **Obesity** is a common disease.
8. _____ **Yipee!** Let's go!
9. _____ Om Puri is **a** marvellous actor.

Nouns may be classified as COUNTABLE and UNCOUNTABLE. Pencils, erasers, books, pens, spoons etc can be counted so they are called Countable. Now consider words like coffee, rice and bread. You cannot count these, so you call them Uncountable Nouns.

1. Look at the list of nouns given : Can you put them under the correct heading?

   information, oranges, thanks, books, salt, paper, box, calendar, ink, bag.

# Nouns

| Countable | Uncountable |
|---|---|
| 1. | 1. |
| 2. | 2. |
| 3. | 3. |
| 4. | 4. |
| 5. | 5. |

**A.** Can you fill in the blanks with apt words to make the sentences meaningful.

1. Govind, please go to Selvan stores and buy me a loaf of _____.
2. "How many litres of _____ do you require Sir?" asked the man at the gas station.
3. Give me a sheet of _____ and I will show you how to make a paper boat.
4. Did you know that you get a bar of _____ with every packet of salted cornflakes?
5. I think this Pulao requires a pinch of _____.

**B.** Match the following :

| 1. | A ball of | cheese |
| 2. | A cube of | music |
| 3. | A slice of | pearls |
| 4. | A pile of | wire |
| 5. | A piece of | stores |
| 6. | A sack of | wheat |
| 7. | A string of | cake |
| 8. | A bottle of | string |

# Noun

1. **Types of Nouns :** Nouns are classified in various ways and usually these classes contrast with one another. For example, Countable Nouns contrast with Uncountable Nouns, Common with Proper.

    a) **Proper Nouns :** These name a specific member of a group. They are always capitalized. **Examples:** Sowmya, India, Cielo.

    b) **Common Nouns :** This is the name given to every person or thing of the same class. **Examples:** Girls, countries, cars.

    c) **Collective Nouns :** These are names of a group considered as a whole. **Examples:** herd, nation, team, committee.

    d) **Abstract Nouns :** These are names of things we cannot perceive with our senses. **Examples:** Democracy, punishment, sadness, speech, theft etc.

    e) **Concrete Nouns :** We can see, hear, taste, touch or smell these nouns. **Examples:** water, silk, pineapple, noise.

    f) **Countable Nouns :** These are the names of separate objects, peoples, ideas etc., that we can count. We use numbers or a/an with countable nouns. They have plurals. **Examples:** a dog, an apple, twenty four sparrows.

    g) **Uncountable Nouns :** These are the names of materials that cannot be counted as separate objects. They have no plurals. We cannot use a/an or a number of with them. **Examples:** Information, music, water, health.

## Exercise - 2

**Directions :** Identify the types of nouns printed boldly in the sentences below. Circle the correct answers.

**Example:**

| Countable | Uncountable | **Travel** broadens the mind. |

| | | | |
|---|---|---|---|
| 1. | Concrete | Abstract | **Honesty** is the best policy |
| 2. | Proper | Common | Mr. **Briggs** was arrested for theft. |
| 3. | Collective | Uncountable | The police dispersed the **crowd**. |
| 4. | Common | Proper | The **soldiers** marched into the valley |
| 5. | Countable | Proper | May I have a glass of **water**. |

Here is a **list of collective nouns.**

| | | | | |
|---|---|---|---|---|
| 1. | Family | | 13. | Government |
| 2. | Team | | 14. | Public |
| 3. | Army | | 15. | Audience |
| 4. | Fury | | 16. | A menagerie of animals |
| 5. | A fleet of ships | | 17. | A posse of policemen |
| 6. | A pride of lions | | 18. | A band of musicians |
| 7. | A galaxy of stars | | 19. | A string of pearls |
| 8. | An anthology of poems | | 20. | A clutch of eggs |
| 9. | A pack of wolves | | 21. | A troupe of dancers |
| 10. | A ream of papers | | 22. | A troop of kangaroos |
| 11. | A pile of notebooks | | 23. | A haul of catch |
| 12. | A sack of potatoes | | 24. | A skulk of foxes |

Here is a **list of countable and uncountable nouns.**

| | Uncountable | Countable |
|---|---|---|
| 1. | Work | a piece of work |
| 2. | Soup | a bowl of soup |
| 3. | Chocolate | a bar of chocolate |

| | | |
|---|---|---|
| 4. | Milk | a jug of milk |
| 5. | Thunder | a clap of thunder |
| 6. | Lightning | a flash of lightning |
| 7. | Grass | a blade of grass |
| 8. | Bread | a loaf / slice of bread |
| 9. | Paper | a piece of sheet paper |
| 10. | Cheese | a cube of cheese / a piece of cheese |
| 11. | Music | a piece / note of music |
| 12. | Rain | a shower of rain |
| 13. | News | a piece of news |
| 14. | Soap | a cake / a bar of soap |
| 15. | Rice | a plate of rice |

## Abstract Noun

| | Adjective | Noun | | Adjective | Noun |
|---|---|---|---|---|---|
| 1. | Long | length | 7. | Efficient | efficiency |
| 2. | Proud | pride | 8. | Magnetic | magnet |
| 3. | Humble | humility | 9. | Mighty | might |
| 4. | Good | goodness | 10. | National | nation |
| 5. | Wicked | wickedness | 11. | Hard | hardness |
| 6. | Kind | kindness | 12. | Helpful | help |

| | Verb | Noun | | Verb | Noun |
|---|---|---|---|---|---|
| 1. | Discover | discovery | 7. | Choose | choice |
| 2. | Purify | purity | 8. | Breathe | breath |
| 3. | Punish | punishment | 9. | Divide | division |
| 4. | Laugh | laughter | 10. | Execute | execution |
| 5. | Expect | expectation | 11. | Fly | flight |
| 6. | Die | death | 12. | Reserve | reservation |

| Common Noun | Abstract |
|---|---|
| 1. Thief | theft |
| 2. Child | childhood |
| 3. Boy | boyhood |
| 4. Friend | friendship |
| 5. Slave | slavery |
| 6. Leader | leadership |
| 7. pilgrims | pilgrimage |

# Exercise - 3

## Directions :

**Odd Noun out :** In each of the following groups of words, one is out of place because it has nothing to do with the other four. Circle the odd word and state why it is odd.

**Example :** taxi, apple, house, (Kamal). Reason : others are common nouns.

1. gang, swarm, group, child, herd _____.
2. ships, eggs, women, sheep, set, _____.
3. good, warm, imaginary, description, kind _____.
4. cruelty, brave, honest, pious, good _____.
5. luggage, money, research, knowledge, coin _____.

**Activity :** Divide the class into 2 groups, Tom and Jerry. To the Toms, hand out strips of paper with sentences like : "A patient Tom is full of _____. A bright Tom glows in the _____. A guilty Tom should admit his _____.

To the Jerries of the class give strips containing the corresponding abstract forms of the adjectives patience, brightness, guilt. Tom and Jerry should pair up and the children form a line. Some/background music can add to the fun!

# Gender

Gender is a classification of pronouns and nouns according as they refer to male or female sex. 'He' refers to the masculine gender and 'she' to the feminine. 'It' refers to the neuter gender, which is neither masculine nor 'feminine'.

|     | Masculine | Feminine |
| --- | --- | --- |
| 1. | buck | doe |
| 2. | dog | bitch |
| 3. | drone | bee |
| 4. | colt | filly |
| 5. | gander | goose |
| 6. | cock/rooster | hen |
| 7. | gentleman | lady |
| 8. | horse | mare |
| 9. | monk | nun |
| 10. | wizard | witch |
| 11. | host | hostess |
| 12. | steward | stewardess |
| 13. | duke | duchess |
| 14. | seamster | seamstress |
| 15. | sorcerer | sorceress |
| 16. | fox | vixen |
| 17. | man-servant | maid-servant |
| 18. | bull | cow |
| 19. | bachelor | spinster/bachelor girl |
| 20. | widower | widow |
| 21. | lad | lass |

| | | | | |
|---|---|---|---|---|
| 22. | nephew | | | niece |
| 23. | sir | | | madam |
| 24. | lion | | | lioness |
| 25. | tom-cat | | | she-cat |

## Common Gender

| | | | | |
|---|---|---|---|---|
| 1. | baby | | 6. | child |
| 2. | infant | | 7. | adult |
| 3. | servant | | 8. | student |
| 4. | cousin | | 9. | player |
| 5. | patient | | 10. | friend |

## Neuter Gender

| | | | | |
|---|---|---|---|---|
| 1. | plate | | 4. | pen |
| 2. | table | | 5. | sofa |
| 3. | stone | | 6. | drum |

Ships and cars are referred to in the feminine gender.

The ship scraped her sides on the treacherous rocks.

The Moon, the Earth, Neptune, Liberty, Spring, peace, hope, charity etc., take the feminine gender.

# Exercise - 4

## Directions :

**Rewrite these sentences changing the nouns printed in bold to their opposite gender.**

**Example :** The **poet** received the prize from the **Queen**.

**Answer :** The poetess received the prize from the king.

1. The **hero** of this film has an action - packed role.
2. The **doe** walked up to the crystal clear pool of water.

3. The **milkman** is late as usual.
4. The **bride** is from Calcutta and the **bridegroom** from Tamilnadu.
5. The poacher laid a trap for the **cow - elephant**.
6. The **doe** is a **female** deer.
7. Obliex the well loved cartoon character was fond of wild **boar**.
8. Black beauty was a splendid looking **colt**.
9. The **drake** is an endangered species.
10. The **cock-sparrow** fluffed up his feathers.

Although they apply to both men and women there are many nouns which are exclusively masculine. Today we have what is called 'non-sexist' language. This applies to people on the whole :

| | |
|---|---|
| Chairman | Chairperson |
| Mankind | humanity |
| manpower | personnel |
| policemen | police officers |
| businessman | industrialist |
| housewife | homemaker |

## Singular / Plural

Make 12 plural nouns by finding the correct ending inside the petals to complete each word outside.

# Number

Nouns that refer to one thing are **Singular** and those that refer to more than one are **Plural**.

## Ways of forming Plurals

a) The plural of a noun is usually formed by adding 's' to the singular.

**Examples :-**

| Singular | Plural |
|----------|--------|
| Girl | Girls |
| Eye | Eyes |
| Table | Tables |
| Cat | Cats |
| House | Houses |

b) By adding 'es' to the singular. Nouns ending in ch, sh, ss, o, x and z form their plurals in this way.

| Singular | Plural |
|----------|--------|
| Church | Churches |
| Dish | dishes |
| Pass | passes |
| Hero | heroes |
| Fox | foxes |
| Waltz | waltzes |

## Exceptions :

Piano – pianos, dynamo – dynamos, bamboo – bamboos, memento – mementos, eskimo – eskimos, photo – photos

c) If a noun ends in 'y', preceded by a consonant, then it forms the plural by changing the 'y' to 'i' and adding 'es'.

**Example :**

| Singular | | Plural |
|---|---|---|
| lady | – | ladies |
| fly | – | flies |
| company | – | companies |
| family | – | families |
| story | – | stories |

But, if a vowel comes immediately before the final 'y' an 's' is added and the 'y' is unchanged.

| Singular | Plural |
|---|---|
| Day | Days |
| Toy | Toys |
| Monkey | Monkeys |
| Guy | Guys |
| Journey | Journeys |

d) The plural of a noun ending in 'f' or 'fe' is formed by dropping 'f' or 'fe' and adding 'ves'

| life | lives |
|---|---|
| thief | thieves |
| shelf | shelves |
| wife | wives |
| leaf | leaves |

## Exceptions :

jewellery, luggage, machinery, toast, apparatus, clothing. (you may say pieces of jewellery, there are three pieces of luggage and would like some toast or 2 pieces of toast, items of clothing, pieces of equipment etc.) chief – chiefs, proof – proofs, dwarf – dwarfs, gulf – gulfs, roof – roofs

e) **Irregular plurals**

| Singular | Plural | Singular | Plural |
|---|---|---|---|
| Foot | Feet | Man | men |
| Mouse | Mice | Louse | lice |
| Goose | Geese | Ox | oxen |
| Woman | Women | Child | children |
| Tooth | teeth | | |

f) **Some nouns are the same in the singular and plural form.**

Deer, sheep, fish, salmon, dozen, score, hundred, thousand stationery, staff, equipment, paint, medicine, soap etc.,

g) **Some nouns are always used in the plural sense :**

scissors, shears, bellows, trousers, measles, people, poultry, cattle, caroms, billiards, means, gallows, police, Jeans, shorts, spectacles.

h) Here are the **plural forms of words borrowed from Greek, Latin and other languages.**

| | |
|---|---|
| bandit | Banditti |
| radius | Radii |
| formula | formulas/formulae |
| axis | axes |
| oasis | oases |
| crisis | crises |
| terminus | termini |
| vertebra | vertebrae / vertebras |
| fungus | fungi |
| medium | media |
| datum | data |

Both 'media' and 'data' are plural forms. They should be used with plural forms of verbs. (e.g.) The mass media have a tremendous influence over the minds of the people.

'Data' is often treated as a singular noun. (e.g.) The data is now available.

**Here are some plural compound nouns:-**

| Singular | | Plural |
|---|---|---|
| passer - by | — | passers - by |
| step - daughter | — | step - daughters |
| son - in - law | — | sons - in - law |
| man - servant | — | men - servants |
| on – looker | — | on - lookers |
| cupful | — | cupfuls |
| handful | — | handfuls |

**Plurals** of symbols, signs, figures and letters are formed by adding 'S'.

| P | P'S |
|---|---|
| MLA | MLA'S |
| 5 | 5's |

## Forming Possessives

The apostrophe (') is used to show possession. When a noun is singular add apostrophe before s. When plural, add an apostrophe after the s.

**Examples :**   This spring's fashions

Saturday's TV serial

Ram's mother

| boss | — | boss's (wife) |
| class | — | class's (reunion) |
| boys | — | the boys' (cycles) |
| girls | — | girls' (skirts) |
| Moses | — | Moses' (laws) |

The preposition 'of' is used when the possession is a thing.

## Add :

a ball of wool, a sum of money, a gust of wind, clouds of smoke, a litre of petrol, a tuft of hair, blade of grass, a metre of cloth, a pot of tea, a piece of burfi.

## Abstract Nouns :

1. The ice melted in the _____ of the sunshine. (warm)
2. There was absolute _____ inside the cave. (dark)
3. Don't creep up behind me like that! You gave me a _____ (fear)

## A convoy of trucks - collective noun

The class made more noise than a gaggle of geese.

## Directions :

Circle the nouns in the sentences below. The number of nouns in each sentence is to be indicated in parentheses.

Example :-

**Jurassic Park** is a fantastic science fiction **film.** (2)

1. This book is dedicated to Gopy, whose intelligence, courage and enthusiasm have been a constant inspiration.
2. Renuka traced her ancestry back to the golden age of the Guptas.
3. The clowns in the circus ring are funny.
4. If you want to grow tall, play basket ball.
5. Though mankind has achieved incalculable progress in science and technology, the mind of man is still polluted with greed, envy and selfishness.
6. The legs of the chair
7. The roof of the hut.

## Exercise - 5

**Find the plurals of the following :**

**Example :** alms     alms

1. Bacterium     _____
2. cactus     _____
3. nucleus     _____
4. sheep     _____
5. stimulus     _____
6. yourself     _____
7. index     _____
8. tornado     _____
9. daughter - in - law     _____
10. piano     _____

## Exercise - 6

**Directions :**

**Rewrite, using an apostrophe to show possession :**

**Example :** The wings of the bird.   The bird's wings.

1. The credit cards of the managers     _____
2. The colour of the flowers     _____
3. The dog of the children     _____
4. The costumes of the participants     _____
5. The plots of the crimes     _____
6. The ears of the elephant     _____

## Exercise - 7

**Directions :**

Some of these sentences are right and some are wrong. Correct the sentences that are wrong. Write 'O.K' if the sentence is correct.

**Example :**

1. Physic is an easy subject. × **Physics is an easy subject.**
2. I have two childs, one girl and one boy.
3. The sheeps are being shorn of their wool.
4. Where are the scissors?
5. They purchased 2 dozens oranges
6. The passer - bys were shocked.
7. I need a new pair of ears.
8. She is a nice people.
9. Her hair is full of louses.
10. Please buy me a trouser.

**Activity :** Write a story that is exactly 80 words long. Your tale must include (1) article a + a word which starts with a vowel. (2) article an + a word which does not start with a vowel. (3) article the + an uncountable noun (4) a plural countable noun without an article before it. Supply a suitable title.

## Adjectives

Adjectives describe nouns and pronouns. They may be classified as:

a) **Proper Adjectives :**
Russian, American, Chinese, Japanese

b) **Adjectives of quality :** little, huge (garden), nice (colour), kind (lady), good (man), beautiful (house)

c) **Adjectives of quantity :**
same, little, much, enough,

d) **Adjectives of number :**
first, second, third, all, a few, several, many, some.

e) **Demonstrative Adjectives :**
This (dog), that (box), those (pencils), these (girls), such (men).

f) **Distributive Adjectives :**
each (boy), every (girl), either, neither.

g) **Interrogative Adjectives :**
Which (child), what (task), whose (book).

h) **Possessive Adjectives :**
my (watch), his (pen), our (child), their (buffallo), your (cow).

i) **Present and Past Participles functioning as adjectives.**

**burnt** (hut), **running** (water)

Adjectives are usually placed before the nouns they describe.

**Example :** Despite the **heavy** rains **many** people were not wearing rain coats.

Adjectives can be formed from nouns and other parts of speech.

| Acid | Acidic | Poison | poisonous |
| Affection | affectionate | Stone | stony |
| Blood | bloody | Coward | cowardly |
| Centre | central | Boy | boyish |
| Magnet | magnetic | Hope | hopeful |

Adjectives follow a fixed order : Colour, origin, material, purpose noun. **Example :** She wore a bunch of red French lace to match with her ball gown.

She filled the big brown earthen pot with water.

## Exercise - 8

### Directions :

From the given list select an adjective that best describes :

1. Someone who is liked and admired.
2. Someone who is not able to articulate his feelings.
3. Someone who throws a party.

4. Someone who talks excessively.
5. Someone who is suitable or qualified for some post.
6. A hard - working person.
7. A person who eats excessively.

diligent, garrulous, host, tongue-tied, popular, eligible, glutton.

## Exercise - 9

## Directions :-

**Match the animal with its symbolic quality :**

**Example :** ant - frugal

| Ass | wise | eagle | graceful |
| Bat | cunning | fox | greedy |
| bear | loyal | kitten | silly, timid |
| bee | cringing | owl | blind |
| bull | industrious | pig | deceitful |
| cat | overbearing | sheep | hypocritical |
| cock | majestic | swan | strong |
| crocodile | playful | worm | stupid |
| dog | ill-tempered | | |

## Note :

A common error when using adjectives is, using 'a' after **kind of** or **'sort of'**.

**Wrong :** I don't like that kind of a dress

**Right :** I don't like that kind of dress

**Adjectives have three degrees of comparison. The positive, comparative and superlative.** The positive degree expresses the quality or characteristic. **Example :** good, nice, short. The comparative degree expresses a degree higher or lower than the positive. **Example :** better, nicer, shorter. The superlative degree expresses the highest or lowest degree of the quality or characteristic. **Example :** the best, the nicest, the shortest.

| (one) | (two) | (more than two) |
|---|---|---|
| **Positive** | **Comparative** | **Superlative** |
| sad | sadder | saddest |
| happy | happier | happiest |
| tall | taller | tallest |
| young | younger | youngest |
| long | longer | longest |
| wise | wiser | wisest |
| good | better | best |
| bad | worse | worst |
| little | less | least |
| much | more | most |
| melodious | more melodious | most melodious |
| beautiful | more beautiful | most beautiful |

The Comparative degree is used when two persons or things are being compared. Example : I think Susmita Sen is more beautiful than Iswarya Rai. In the sentence Comparative degree word 'than' is used.

When 3 or more persons or things are being compared, the superlative degree is used. 'The' is used before superlatives.
**Example :** Meera is the tallest girl in the class.

## Exercise - 10

**Directions :**

Insert the correct degree of the adjective given in brackets.

**Example :** He is the stouter of the two boys. (stout)

1. Sing a little _____, please. (loud)

2. The pen is _____ than the sword. (mighty)
3. Hope you are feeling _____ today! (well)
4. How much _____ do I have to walk? (far)
5. Carl Lewis is the _____ runner of this decade. (fast)
6. America is the _____ country in the world. (rich)

## Exercise - 11

**Directions :**

**Rewrite each sentence using the correct form of the adjective :**

**Example :** I think this is the most laziest boy, I have ever seen. ×
I think this is the laziest boy I have ever seen.

1. Which is the lightest of the two boxes?
2. Of all the sums, this is simple.
3. Raj is more cleverer than Vicky.
4. Her cold became worser.
5. Which is the worse, caning, or imposition?

Here are **3 ways of saying the same thing :**

**Superlative :** The Vedas are the best sources of wisdom.

**Comparative :** The Vedas are better than any other source of wisdom.

**Positive :** No other source of wisdom is so good as the Vedas.

## Exercise - 12

**Directions :**

Rewrite each of these sentences by changing the degree of comparison, without changing the meaning. You may refer to the chart given at the end of the exercise.

1. Barbie is the prettiest doll in the toy shop.
2. AIDS is the deadliest of all diseases.

3. This is the happiest day of my life.
4. The Rolls Royce is the most expensive car.
5. Dharini is smarter than Nithya.
6. Mrs. Narayan is one of the nicest people I have ever met.
7. Artole is the most marvellous cook, in the world.
8. Dr. Sundarrajan is the most skilful of all surgeons in Chennai.
9. This red flask is better than that green one.
10. Mount Everest is the highest peak in the world.
11. Example is the greatest teaching aid.
12. Love is the scarcest article today.

**Activity :** Blindfold a student. Give him objects like a pebble, water bottle, school bag, plastic toys, soft toys etc. Ask questions like : Is hot or cold? big or small? smooth or rough? Tell the child to describe the object. **Example :** This sweet is smooth, chewy, round and soft.

Show the students pictures of national leaders and ask them to describe them in one or two apt words.

Adjectives can be used to make comparison.

Ram is fat.

Shyam is fatter than Ram.

Nataraj is the fattest of the three.

## Degrees of Comparison

| Positive | Comparative | Superlative |
|---|---|---|
| (One) | (Two) | (More than two) |
| Heavy | Heavier | Heaviest |
| Bright | Brighter | Brightest |
| Tall | Taller | Tallest |
| Great | Greater | Greatest |
| Easy | Easier | Easiest |

| | | |
|---|---|---|
| Good | Better | Best |
| Bad | Worse | Worst |
| Little | Less | Least |
| Many, Much | More | Most |
| | | |
| Practical | More practical | Most practical |
| Beautiful | More beautiful | Most beautiful |
| Sensible | More sensible | Most sensible |
| Colourful | More colourful | Most colourful |
| Generous | More generous | Most generous |
| | | |
| Top | | Topmost |
| Bottom | | Bottommost |

## Note :

The Comparative Degree is followed by 'than'.

The Superlative Degree is preceded by 'the'.

**Interchange of Degrees of Comparison :**

Good,

Positive : No other -------- so good as

Comparative : Better than any other

Superlative : The best

Positive : No other boy in the class is **so tall as** Ranjit.

Comparative : Ranjit is **taller than** any other boy in the class.

Superlative : Ranjit is **the tallest boy** in the class.

Positive : Some .................... at least as good as

Comparative : Not better than some

Superlative : Not the best

| | |
|---|---|
| Positive | : Some girls in the class are at least **as smart as** Rita. |
| Comparative | : Rita is not **smarter than** some girls of the class. |
| Superlative | : Rita is not **the smartest** girl in the class. |
| Positive | : Very few ...... as good as |
| Comparative | : Better than most |
| Superlative | : One of the best |
| Positive | : Very few batsmen in India are **as skilful as** Tendulkar. |
| Comparative | : Tendulkar is more **skilful than** most batsmen in India. |
| Superlative | : Tendulkar is one of **the most skilful** batsmen in India. |
| Positive | : Not so good as some others |
| Comparative | : Some better than |
| Superlative | : Not one of the best |
| Positive | : Mumbai is not **as big as** some cities of India. |
| Comparative | : Some cities of India are **bigger than** Mumbai. |
| Superlative | : Mumbai is not one of **the biggest** cities of India. |
| Positive | : Crackle is not **so crunchy as** Cadbury's fruit and Nut. |
| Comparative | : Cadbury's fruit and Nut is **crunchier** than crackle. |
| Superlative | : (Here superlative is not possible since only two things are being compared). |

## Exercise - 12A

**Directions :**

**Rewrite the following sentences in the positive degree :**

1. Black holes are the most mysterious phenomenon in the universe.
2. White popcorn is blander than masala popcorn.
3. Naveen is more organized than the other students.
4. This was the most valuable contribution ever donated.
5. There is less sugar in this tin than in that one.

## Directions :

**Rewrite using the comparative degree :**

1. The sword is not as mighty as the pen.
2. Rahim is not as short as Ram.
3. No other metal is as useful as iron.
4. Sylvia is not as modest as the other girls in her group.
5. His drawings are as good as Jennifer's.

## Directions :

**Give the other degrees of comparison :**

1. Man is harder than iron, stronger than stone and more fragile than a rose.
2. Ranjit is the tallest boy in the class.
3. Silk is smoother than cotton.
4. Atal Behari Vajpayee is one of the most charismatic leaders that India has ever produced.
5. Tendulkar is the most skilful batsman in the world.

### WORDS THAT GO TOGETHER

Pros and Cons (Advantages and Disadvantages) Alpha and Omega (The beginning and the end) Crime and Punishment

Yes and No

# Determiners

Determiners identify nouns. They point them out. Example : The, this, that, what etc.,

**Kinds of Determiners.**

1. Articles :-     A, An, The
2. Demonstratives :-     This, that, there, these
3. Distributive :-     Either, neither, each, every
4. Possessive :-     My, ours, your, his, her, its, their

5. Quantitative :- Much, little, whole, half, some, any, enough, all, sufficient, no, none.
6. Numeral :- One, two, first, second, third etc.
7. Interrogative :- What, which, where.

## Articles

**Indefinite article :** a/an

**Definite article :** the

    a) We use 'a' or an before singular countable nouns.
       a bag, a plane, a book, an ant, an experiment, an umbrella.

    b) Words beginning with a consonant sound.
       a one day match, a European, a university

    c) 'an' before words with a 'vowel' sound. an M.P., an honest lady, an hotel.

1. 'The' before a countable or uncountable noun already refered to
**Example :** the plane I arrived by ; the book you gave me.
2. Before the names of bays, gulfs, rivers, seas, oceans, group of islands, mountain ranges, ships, deserts, trains, aeroplanes, newspapers, famous buildings, countries, whole families and certain books.

| | |
|---|---|
| Bays | : The bay of Bengal |
| Gulf | : The gulf of Mexico |
| Rivers | : The Brahmaputra; The Ganga |
| Seas and Oceans | : The Arabian sea, The Pacific. |
| Islands | : The West Indies |
| Mountain Ranges | : The Himalayas, The Vindhyas |
| Ships | : The Titanic |
| Deserts | : The Sahara |
| Trains | : The Shatabdi Express; The Coromandel |

| | |
|---|---|
| Aeroplane | : The concorde ; The Jumbo Jet |
| Newspapers | : The Hindu ; The Indian Express |
| Famous buildings | : The Kuthubminar ; The Lotus Temple |
| Countries | : The U.K. ; The United States of America |
| Whole families | : The Gandhis ; The Tatas ; The Birlas |
| Books | : The Vedas ; The Ramayana ; The Odyssey; The Iliad. |

3. Before a singular noun used to represent a class :
   The cockroach has survived on this earth for millions of years.
4. Before the superlative degree. Kirthivasan is the tallest boy in the class.
5. In certain instances before the comparative
   Radha is the better dancer of the two.
   The more the merrier.
   The harder you work the sooner you'll finish digging the pit.
6. Before adjectives of quality when it is used as a noun.
   Blessed are the poor and the meek
7. Before ordinals like first, second, third.
   Kasturi bagged the first prize in inter-school singing competition.
8. We say the radio, the theatre, the cinema but we omit 'the' with reference to television. 'I love watching television.'
   **But :** Please switch off the T.V. (Here you are referring to the set).
9. We do not use articles with proper nouns, material nouns, names of meals, diseases, names of days, months and seasons and with several verbal phrases. eg. :
   Vikram Seth is a marvellous poet.
   Not the Vikram Seth
   The price of gold has gone down
   Not the gold.
   Eat breakfast like an emperor, lunch like a king and dinner like a pauper.

Not the breakfast ......
AIDS is a killer disease
Not the AIDS
English is a flexible language
Not the English. The English refers to the English people.
'The' should be omitted in some phrases.

**Example :** Go to bed, go to hospital, go to prison, go home, go by bus - car - air - sea - on foot - to school - church - court, on earth, dawn to dusk, in jail.

'The' should be omitted with words like father, mother aunt, etc.
**Example :** Mother is out shopping and father is working on his PC.

## Exercise - 13

### Directions :

**Fill in the blanks with 'a', 'an', or 'the'.**

1. What _____ lovely salwar kameez!
2. His batting was in _____ shambles.
3. I like the music of _____ falling rain.
4. The Indian cricket team will be staying at _____ Grand Hotel.
5. I would love to learn to play _____ cello.
6. It is _____ shame, the way _____ terrorists are dominating Kashmir.
7. You are asked to come for _____ interview on _____ 21st of January.
8. He drove at forty kilometres _____ hour.
9. B.V. Raman is _____ astrologer.

# Exercise - 14

## Directions :

Rewrite the following sentences in their correct form :

    Example :    (i)    1. Can you fly plane?
                              Ans : Can you fly a plane?

                 (ii)   B.V. Raman is a astrologer
                        Ans : B.V. Raman is an astrologer.

1. Would you like cup of tea?
2. Sri Lanka is island.
3. I found an one rupee coin on the pavement.
4. More we have more we desire.
5. She is electronics engineer.
6. I have to consult orthopaedic surgeon for my fracture.
7. I like to watch the television.
8. Milk is sold by litre.
9. Read Ramayana and come closer to Divine.
10. Indian Express is one of the leading newspapers.
11. Let there be peace on the earth.
12. The Aluminium is an useful metal.

## Demonstratives :

    This, That, These, Those. They are used with nouns. This and that are used with singular nouns, those and 'these' with plural.

    **Examples :** Don't eat those guavas. They are rotten. I hate these shoes. They are so tight. Who lives in that house? This plate is not clean.

## Exercise - 15

**Directions :**

Insert this or these in the blanks :

1. _____ shirt.
2. _____ children
3. _____ shirts.
4. _____ pizzas
5. _____ table.
6. _____ student.

**Directions :**

Put in that or those :

1. _____ flowers.
2. _____ picture.
3. _____ shoes.
4. _____ eggs.
5. _____ peacock.
6. _____ tigers.

## Possessives :

my, our, your, his, her, its, their, are possessives. We use them before singular and plural nouns. (The possessive form + 's is used for people and animals. It is not generally used for things. **Example :** The cook's ladle, the queen's tiara, the dog's tail. But we say, "the pages of the book". "the handle - bar of the cycle". (The 's is used with nouns denoting time, space or weight. **Example :** A week's, holiday's, a stone's throw).

## Exercise - 16

**Directions :**

Insert my/our/your/his/her/their/its.

1. Shantiniketan is famous for _____ Vishwabarthi university.
2. The dog wagged _____ tail.
3. Is Rita _____ best friend?
4. _____ husband works in a bank.

5. _____ favourite game is cricket.

6. _____ lover's name is Doddi.

7. _____ children study in Chettinad Vidhyashram.

8. _____ son writes beautiful poems.

9. I met them yesterday but I cannot recollect _____ names.

10. We are going to invite _____ friends to the house-warming.

## Distributives :

either, neither, each, every

We use either/neither to talk about 2 things or people. They are used with singular nouns. Either can mean both or any one.

**Example :** (i) Beautiful rose bushes have been planted on either side of the lane.

(ii) You may either come with us to the movies or stay at home.

Neither means not one or the other.

Ram is not coming, Me neither.

Neither pen writes well.

## Directions :

**Insert either/neither in the blanks :**

1. Are you a Tamilian or a Malayalee? _____ I am a Bengali.

2. I have bought a doughnut and a pastry. Which one do you want? _____ I just want something sweet.

3. Which ice cream do you prefer? Rasberry, duet or coconut? _____ I hate icecreams.

4. This chart is great. I guess _____ Padmini or Smiline has put it up.

5. We didn't eat _____ of us was hungry.

6. Do you want us to play classical music or pop? You can have _____

7. I can _____ play the Veena nor the Violin.
8. I _____ smoke nor drink.
9. I go to school _____ by car or on foot.
10. _____ Ahmed or Benhur must have committed the crime.

## each / every

We are each when we think of things separately one by one, 'Every' refers to things in a group without exception. **Example :** Each child was given a banana. Every student in this class is talented. When we use each and every to describe the subject of a sentence, the verb relating to the subject is singular.

## Directions :

**Fill in the blanks with each/every.**

1. I buy new sarees by the dozen _____ year when the grand reduction sale is on.
2. The children were given a packet of firecrackers _____
3. Take _____ day as it comes.
4. _____ country has a national anthem.
5. _____ of the apples in the box was slightly rotten.
6. _____ side of the square is of equal length.

## Quantifiers :

some, any, much, no, none, many, several, a lot of, sufficient, enough, few, all etc.

**Some, any :** 'Some' has a positive connotation, while 'any' is usually negative. **Example :** Chop some onions for upma.

There isn't any tea left. In most questions we use 'any'. Don't you have any commonsense? We use 'some' when we offer or ask for things. Would you have some tea? Can I borrow some sugar?

## Directions :

**Fill in the blanks with some or any.**

1. Would you like _____ fish? No thanks. I don't want _____.
2. I am going to buy _____ potatoes.
3. There aren't _____ shops on this street.
4. _____ people are rather narrow-minded.
5. Isn't there _____ shampoo? I want to wash my hair.
6. Can you help me? I am having _____ trouble opening this cooker.
7. _____ of my friends hopped in and had a whole of a time last evening.
8. Ranjana and Shyam don't have _____ children so they are planning to adopt a child.
9. I am going for walk. I need _____ fresh air.
10. I cannot take _____ photographs as I have forgotten to buy a roll of film.
11. You may cash this cheque at _____ bank.
12. Buy _____ skirt and you get an umbrella free!

## Much, Many

'Many' is used before countable nouns, and 'much' before uncountables. **Example :** You have not eaten much. Aren't you feeling well? Many are called but only a few are chosen.

## Directions :

**Fill in the blanks with 'much' or 'many'.**

1. _____ of the work was left undone.
2. _____ trees were cut down.
3. _____ students are absent today.
4. She was granted _____ favours.
5. _____ effort is required to win the Olympics.
6. Hurry up. I don't have _____ time.

## Few :

'Few' means not many, almost none.

A few means some.

The few means all in the group.

## Directions :

**Fill in the blanks with few, a few, the few.**

a) _____ children can resist chocolates.

b) The chief guest was asked to speak _____ words.

c) He wrote letters to _____ friends he had.

d) _____ can speak English grammatically.

e) _____ people can keep secrets.

## Little :

Little, a little, the little.

Little means not much or hardly any, negligible.

A little means some, though not much.

The little means not much but all that there is.

## Directions :

**What do these sentences mean?**

1. Radha has little to do with administrative duties.
2. The patient managed to swallow a little fruit juice.
3. A little knowledge is a dangerous thing.
4. The poor man shared the little food he had with the dog.

## Interrogatives :

These help to ask questions and may be used before any kind of noun.

1. **Which** book do you want?
2. **Whose** child are you?
3. **What** sort of pen do you need?

# Pronouns

"People who eat lots of potatoes, white bread and white rice are in the mistaken belief that it is the best way to follow a low-fat diet ; may be doing themselves more harm than good. These increase blood glucose levels more than eating sugar itself"

The 'Pronoun' Test

Robert Reich used a "pronoun" test to learn about the many companies he visited.

If a front-line worker described a company as "they" or "them", he saw a division separating management and employees.

But if they answered with a "We" or "us", "then" I know I'm in a new world.

Pronouns are generally used in place of nouns or noun phrases already used. They function as nouns. I, you, we, himself, etc. one, ones are pronouns. Can you pick out the pronouns from the above passage?

_____ (refers to) potatoes, white bread and white rice.

_____ (refers to) people.

_____ sugar.

## 1. Kinds of Pronouns :

Pronouns that stand for persons, creatures or things are called **Personal pronouns.**

|  | Singular | Plural |
|---|---|---|
| I Person | I, me | we, us, |
| II Person | You | you, |
| III Person | he, him, she, her, it | They, them |

## Directions :

Use suitable pronouns in this telephone conversation :

Radha :    Hello! May _____ speak to Rajesh?

Vicky :        _____ has gone to watch the India-Pakistan Cricket finals. May _____ know who is calling?

Radha :        _____ am _____ batchmate Radha. Could _____ take down a message for Rajesh?

Vickey :       Oh sure.

Radha :        Please tell _____ that Renuka wants _____ history notes back.

_____ has taken _____ tiffin box with _____ by mistake. _____ contains same yummy gulab jamun.

Do ask _____ to return _____ if _____ has not polished _____ off already.

Vicky :        Right. Bye!

Radha :        Thanks. Bye.

## 2. Reflexive Pronouns :

These are used as the object of a verb and they turn back the action on the subject.

|  | Singular | Plural |
| --- | --- | --- |
| First person | myself | ourselves |
| Second person | yourself | yourselves |
| Third person | himself | themselves |
|  | herself |  |
|  | itself |  |

**Examples :**   1. Maria cut herself with the bread knife.

2. I learnt to operate it myself.

3. They helped themselves with the food.

## 3. Emphatic or Intensive pronouns :

These are used to stress some point. They are always used with a noun or another pronoun that acts as a subject or object.

We ourselves cooked the dinner. I myself saw her stab Stalin D'souza. They themselves confessed to have committed the crime.

## 4. Possessive pronouns :

Mine, yours, his, hers, theirs, its - indicate possession so they are called possessive pronouns.

> **Example :** These Gulab Jamuns of yours are marvellous.
> This box is mine.
> The dog wagged its tail.

## 5. Indefinite pronouns :

someone, somebody, everyone, few, all, many, none are called indefinite pronouns as they do not refer to a particular person or thing.

**Example :** Many of the passengers were injured in the train accident.

Nobody was there to help Nalini.

## Directions :

**Fill in the blanks in the paragraph below with the indefinite pronouns:-**

Nobody, anybody, everybody, somebody.

This is the story of 4 people named _____, _____, _____ and _____. There was an important job to be done and _____ was sure that somebody would do it. _____ could have done it but nobody did it. _____ got annoyed about that because it was everybody's job and _____ thought that anybody could do it. But _____ realised that everybody would not do it. It so happened that _____ blamed somebody when actually _____ accused anybody.

The moral of this tale is _____
_____
_____
_____

## 6. Distributive Pronouns :

Distributive pronouns are used to denote persons or things one at a time. They are always used in the singular and the verb following them must also be singular. Each, Either and Neither are distributive pronouns.

**Example :**  1. Each of these cats has its pedigree.
2. Either of you can go to town.
3. Neither of the ministers is trustworthy.

## Note :

Each, Either and Neither are sometimes used as adjectives.
**Example :** Neither child is speaking the truth. At either side was a lamp-post. Each man cast his vote.

## 7. Interrogative Pronouns :

Who, whom, whose, which, what are called interrogative pronouns. **Example :** Who was that remarkable lady? What are you searching for? Which of your new salwars will you wear for the wedding?

## 8. Demonstrative Pronouns :

This, that, these and those are demonstrative pronouns. They point out people and things. This (singular) and these (plural) refer to people and things nearby. That and those refer to people or things further away.

Demonstrative pronouns refer to things mentioned in previous sentences and they help to introduce ideas and things.

**Example :**  1. This is the blue print I was talking about.
2. Those are priceless.

3. William let off the air from the balloon, making a dreadful noise. **That** annoyed the teacher.

4. **These** are the main issues the BJP has on its agenda.

   1. Stability, 2. Social justice 3. Restoring National Pride.

## Note :

This, that, there and those are adjectives when they are used with a noun. **Example : This book** (noun) is fascinating. 2. **These apples** (noun) are mine.

## 9. Relative Pronoun :

Relative Pronouns are used to link 2 sentences. It always introduces a relative clause. They are who, whom, where, which, that, what. The nouns to which these pronouns refer to are called **antecedents**.

**Example :** 1. This is the house. Govind designed it.
This is the house that Govind designed.

2. The lady who is campaigning for the congress is Sonia Gandhi.

## Directions :

**Identify the boldly printed pronouns in the sentences below using the following code :**

D — Demonstrative Pronoun ;  R — Relative Pronoun ;
IND — Indefinite Pronoun ;  I — Interrogative pronoun.

**Example :**  IND  — Is **everything** Okay?

1. _____ **Who** wants to come to Kishkinta?

2. _____ Alarippu, Shabdam, Varnam, Padam — **These** are words related to Barathanatyam.

3. _____ The Jaipur foot **that** Sudha Chandran acquired, helped her make the historic comeback.

4. _____ Does **anybody** believe that Nethaji Subhas Chandra Bose is still alive.

| | | |
|---|---|---|
| 5. | _____ | He **who** hestitates is lost. |
| 6. | _____ | Alladdin told his mother to sell the old lamp **which** he had brought from the cave. |
| 7. | _____ | **Somebody** has stolen my little green box. |
| 8. | _____ | **What** is wrong with this Radio? |
| 9. | _____ | Communal matters ! **These** are beyond my comprehension. |
| 10. | _____ | **What** is a glitch? |

## 10. Reciprocal Pronouns :

'Each other' and 'one another' are reciprocal pronouns as they express shared feeling or actions.

**Example :** 1. Romeo and Juliet loved each other.

2. The protestants and the catholics fight one another on religious issues.

## Directions :

Identify the errors in each of the following sentences. Write the correct word in the space provided.

**Example :**

They    The pans have copper bottoms so that **it** can be heated faster.

| | | |
|---|---|---|
| 1. | _____ | I have a photograph of my brother playing her own guitar. |
| 2. | _____ | These Tee shirts are for Ashwin and myself. |
| 3. | _____ | Dev and myself enjoy travelling. |
| 4. | _____ | Students ! Work out these sums yourself. |
| 5. | _____ | The lady to who I gave the money had vanished. |
| 6. | _____ | I wish I could find sarees as attractive as your's. |

7. _____ Who's cap is this?
8. _____ Your one of the best cricketers I have ever seen.
9. _____ Dad told Santhosh and I to be down in 5 minutes.
10. _____ Us Animal lovers are very happy with Menaka Gandhi.
11. _____ Susmita is better looking than me.
12. _____ Everybody should brush their teeth twice a day.
13. _____ Both the girls forgot her ID cards.
14. _____ Either Seema or Radha left their water bottle behind in the staff room.
15. _____ A.R. Rehman's 'Vande Mataram' is as popular abroad as they are here.

# Verbs

A verb is a word that expresses an action or a state of being. Verbs can be classified as **principal (main) verbs**. These are action verbs, expressing physical or mental actions like : Write, eat, see, go, feel, come, hope, talk, dance, desire.

Verbs like be, grow, appear, look, seem, smell, see, taste, become, feel, express a condition or state of being. These verbs connect the subject to the nouns or adjectives in the sentence.

Linking verbs include all forms of the verb to be : am, is, are, was and were. do, have, can, may, must, will, shall are called **Auxiliary or helping verbs.** They always accompany one or more other verbs. Example : Don't go there. Have you anything to say?

## Note :

An adjective follows a linking verb.

Example : 1. The plan sounds good.

2. I feel miserable.

## Kinds of Main Verbs

A **transitive verb** may take a direct or an indirect object. **It expresses an action that is performed on an object.** A direct object receives the action. If you ask the question whom? or what? to an action word and find the answer in the same sentence, the verb is transitive.

Example : Mrs. Rajan **bought** (verb) an enormous water bucket.

The answer to the question bought what? is - an enormous water bucket. So 'bought' is a transitive verb.

Example : Steffi hits **the ball.** 'the ball' is the direct object.

An indirect object names the thing or the person for whom the action is performed. Example : Mrs. Saroja gave her daughter an exquisite Ganesha on Pongal Day. Here, the **Indirect Object** is **daughter** and the **direct object** is **Ganesha.**

Intrasitive Verbs are not followed by direct objects. Example : I walk to school everyday. Walk what? No answer. But **I walk my dog every day. Walk what?** - dog (direct object) so here walk is a transitive verb. So, a verb may be transitive or intransitive depending on how it is used.

More examples :

| Transitive | Intransitive |
|---|---|
| He **stopped** the train | The train **stopped** |
| Lilly **rang** the bell | The **bell** rang |
| Alisa **sang** a pop song. | Alisa **sang** in the school choir. |

## Verb Forms

| Present | Past | Past Participle |
|---|---|---|
| abide | abode | abode |
| awake | awoke | awoke |
| arise | arose | arisen |
| bear | bore | borne (born) |
| beat | beat | beaten |
| begin | began | begun |
| behold | beheld | beheld (beholden) |
| bid | bid (bade) | bidden |
| bind | bound | bound |
| blow | blew | blown |
| choose | chose | chosen |
| cling | clung | clung |
| come | came | come |
| crow | crew (crowed) | crowed |
| dig | dug (digged) | dug (digged) |

| | | |
|---|---|---|
| do | did | done |
| draw | drew | drawn |
| eat | ate | eaten |
| fall | fell | fallen |
| fight | fought | fought |
| find | found | found |
| fly | flew | flown |
| forget | forgot | forgotten |
| forsake | forsook | forsaken |
| freeze | froze | frozen |
| get | got | got (gotten) |
| give | gave | given |
| go | went | gone |
| grind | ground | ground |
| grow | grew | grown |
| hang | hung (hanged) | hung (hanged) |
| hold | held | held |
| know | knew | known |
| lie | lay | lain |
| ride | rode | ridden |
| ring | rang | rung |
| rise | rose | risen |
| see | saw | seen |
| shake | shook | shaken |
| shine | shone | shone |
| shrink | shrank | shrunk |

| | | |
|---|---|---|
| sing | sang | sung |
| sit | sat | sat |
| slay | slew | slain |
| speak | spoke | spoken |
| spin | spun | spun |
| spring | sprang | sprung |
| stand | stood | stood |
| steal | stole | stolen |
| stick | stuck | stuck |
| sting | stung | stung |
| strive | strove | striven |
| swim | swam | swum |
| take | took | taken |
| tear | tore | torn |
| throw | threw | thrown |
| wake | woke | woke |
| wear | wore | worn |
| weave | wove | woven |
| win | won | won |
| wind | wound | wound |
| wring | wrung | wrung |
| write | wrote | written |

**Weak verbs shorten the vowel in the past tense**

| | | |
|---|---|---|
| bleed | bled | bled |
| breed | bred | bred |
| creep | crept | crept |

| | | |
|---|---|---|
| deal | dealt | dealt |
| dream | dreamt | dreamt |
| feed | fed | fed |
| feel | felt | felt |
| flee | fled | fled |
| keep | kept | kept |
| kneel | knelt | knelt |
| lead | led | led |
| leave | left | left |
| lose | lost | lost |
| mean | meant | meant |
| meet | met | met |
| read | read | read |
| say | said | said |
| shoot | shot | shot |
| sleep | slept | slept |
| sweep | swept | swept |
| weep | wept | wept |

**Weak verbs that have the same form in the past tense.**

| | | |
|---|---|---|
| rid | rid | rid |
| cut | cut | cut |
| set | set | set |
| put | put | put |

# WEAK VERBS (with the same Past, Past Participle form)

| | | |
|---|---|---|
| beseech | besought | besought |
| bring | brought | brought |

| buy   | bought            | bought            |
|-------|-------------------|-------------------|
| catch | caught            | caught            |
| seek  | sought            | sought            |
| teach | taught            | taught            |
| tell  | told              | told              |
| think | thought           | thought           |
| work  | worked (wrought)  | worked (wrought)  |

## Lie and Lay

**'Lie'** means to tell an untruth. It also means to recline.

1. People could not believe that the president had lied.
2. I feel giddy. Let me lie down for a few minutes. After I lay down, I felt better. 'Lie' is an intransitive verb.

**Lay** means to put down.

Hens lay eggs.

She laid the table.

The verb 'lay' is transitive.

## Directions :

Pick the verbs from the following sentences and say whether they are transitive or Intransitive.

### Example :

<u>Transitive</u>  Uma's grand daughter **visited** her last month.

1. _____ Rajesh always leaves books, papers and pencils on the dining table.
2. _____ Vikram built a cardboard model of the Red Fort.
3. _____ Set the table, please.

4. _____ Ladies and gentlemen, please sit down.
5. _____ The baby lying in the cradle is gurgling away in joy.
6. _____ Meena looks beautiful in her polka-dotted dress.
7. _____ The clock chimed ten.
8. _____ Thousands attended Lata Mangeshkar's music festival.
9. _____ The Moghuls and the British zealots could not destroy Hinduism.
10. _____ Yasodha smiled at the infant Krishna.

## Regular and Irregular Verbs

Every verb has 3 main parts. The present, the past and the past participle. Regular verbs form the past and past participle by adding 'd' or 'ed' to the present. The participle always takes a helping verb.

| Present | Past    | Past Participle |
|---------|---------|-----------------|
| clean   | cleaned | cleaned         |
| live    | lived   | lived           |
| study   | studied | studied         |
| paint   | painted | painted         |
| talk    | talked  | talked          |

## Irregular Verbs

| Present         | Past      | Past Participle |
|-----------------|-----------|-----------------|
| arise           | arose     | arisen          |
| be (am, is, are)| was/were  | been            |
| bite            | bit       | bitten          |
| go              | went      | gone            |
| write           | wrote     | written         |
| bring           | brought   | brought         |

| | | |
|---|---|---|
| broadcast | broadcast | broadcast |
| burn | burnt, burned | burnt, burned |
| bleed | bled | bled |
| bend | bent | bent |
| beat | beat | beaten |
| become | became | became |
| break | broke | broken |
| build | built | built |
| cry | cried | cried |
| cut | cut | cut |
| fly | flew | flown |
| forgive | forgave | forgiven |
| light | lighted, lit | lighted, lit |
| lie | lay | lain |
| lay | laid | laid |
| hurt | hurt | hurt |
| freeze | froze | frozen |
| hide | hid | hidden |
| hit | hit | hit |
| eat | ate | eaten |
| dream | dreamed, dreamt | dreamed, dreamt |
| do | did | done |
| pay | paid | paid |
| say | said | said |
| ride | rode | ridden |
| spring | sprang | sprung |
| speak | spoke | spoken |

| sew | sewed | sewn, sewed |
| take | took | taken |
| choose | chose | chosen |
| know | knew | known |
| weave | wove | woven |

### 1. Auxiliary Verbs :

**Be :** to be, am, is, are, was, were, been, being – is used in progressive tense (Active voice) forms.

    I am playing.

    He is playing.

    They are playing.

    She was playing.

    They were playing.

    I shall be playing.

### 2. It is used in all Passive Voice Forms :

    I am examined.
    He is examined.
    They are examined.
    He was examined.
    We were examined.
    He will be examined.
    He has been examined.
    He is being examined.

### 3. Be as a Main Verb :

    I am thrilled.
    We are thrilled.
    He is thrilled.
    They were thrilled.
    Rajan is thrilled.

4. **Negative sentences :**

   I am not going to the party.
   He is not going to the party.
   They are not going to the party.
   We are not going to the party.
   I shall not be going to the party.

5. **Interrogative sentences :**

   Are they coming to the filmshow?
   Am I invited?
   Is the president speaking the truth?
   Was it predicted?

6. **Other uses :**

   He **is** to leave immediately.
   They **are** to be arrested.
   She is about to weep.
   I am not invited but my sister is.

# Have

to have, have, has, had, having
Have + past participle = perfect tenses.
How long have you been married?
I have done it.
He has eaten it.
She had seen the movie already.
He has been in Canada since July.

## Negatives :

I have not spoken to her as yet.
She had not spoken to her as yet.
He has not spoken to her as yet.

**Have as a main verb :**

    I have the documents.

    She had a car.

**Other uses :**

    Have you made some coffee?

    She had to do it.

    You had better get going.

    You had better not miss writing the exam.

**Do :**

    to do, do, does, did, doing, done

**Do** is used to form negative and interrogative sentences in Present Simple and Past Simple.

**Example :**    I do not smoke or drink.

              He does not know to read or write.

    Did you complete your home work?

    What was Rinku doing when you saw her?

**Do as a main verb.**

    He did it!

    Do is used in short answers.

    Do you take this man to be your lawfully wedded husband? **I do**

    Does your man know? He does

    Did she speak to you? She **didn't**

    **Done** like all past participles is used with has, have, had, be, been, being.

    The task is done.

## Activity (Helping Verbs)

    Form 2 teams. Team X will ask the questions first. It will secretly write the name of a famous personality on a piece of paper and give it to the teacher. Team X will now ask questions beginning with 'Did', do or does, has or is

**Example :**   Has he won the Bharath Ratna?

Did he fight for the country?

Does his name begin with a B?

The other team should answer Yes or No. The team that guesses the answer by asking the least number of questions is the winner.

## Modal Auxiliaries :

can, could, may, might, must, ought, shall, should, will and would are called **modal auxiliaries.** They express a wide range of meanings and are used with basic forms of verbs. They are not influenced by the subject.

Can (Present), could (Past) indicate ability, possibility

I can skate.

She can go to Tokyo.

Peter cannot speak French.

(**Note :** Cannot is written as one word)

**May :**

May is used to express possibility.

He may come on Sunday.

Permission   :   May I go now?

Wishes         :   May God bless India!

**Must :**

Must indicates necessity. Must I sing on stage? You must write your name on top of the page.

**Will :**

Will indicates future time :   I will meet him next week.
**Request :** Will you shut the window, please?
**Determination :** I will quit smoking.

**Need :**

Need is used in negative sentences : You need not carry those books.
**Interrogative sentences** : Do you need help?

**Would** the past tense of will is used to express past habits. The canary would sing everyday.

**As an invitation :** Would you like to come into my parlour?

**Polite requests :** I would like some tea, please. Would you give Anita this parcel?
Would is used instead of shall/will when the reporting verb is in the past tense.

**Example :**

**Direct :** He said, "I shall/will bring it".

**Indirect :** He said he would bring it.
Would you mind ..... is an expression used for asking permission.
Would you mind opening this bottle?

**Should** is used with the conjunction 'lest.'

He studied hard lest he should fail. If the reporting verb is in the past tense, 'shall' is changed to should while changing it into indirect speech.

Should is a milder word than must. Another way of saying should is 'ought to'. I don't think you ought to watch TV till two in the morning.

**Ought to :** This expresses obligation with much emphasis.

1. You look very pale. I think you ought to see a doctor.
2. You are diabetic. You ought not to eat sweets.

**Dare :** This word implies challenge, or courage. It can be used as a main verb, an auxiliary in negative sentences, in interrogative sentences and to express probability.

1. I dare you to walk on the parapet wall. (main)
2. With the thief holding the pistol against the nape of my neck, **I dare** not move. (auxiliary)

3. My lips are sealed. I dare not reveal the names of those involved in the Bofors kickback case.
4. How dare you look at me like that?
   Did he dare ask for the hand of the princess? (Interrogative).
5. I dare say tomorrow will be a holiday on account of the heavy rain. (probability)

**Used to :** This indicates some constant or frequent practice in the past. With be forms it means getting accustomed. **Example :** I used to drink 10 glasses of water every morning. The noise does not bother me. I am used to it.

## Directions :

**Fill in the blanks with appropriate modals.**

1. If I had a lakh of rupees, I _____ go for a trip round the world.
2. Raj is ambidexterous. He _____ write with both hands.
3. _____ I have another helping of the fruit salad please?
4. Wear your raincoat. It _____ start pouring soon according to the weather forecast.
5. You _____ take better care of your aged aunt.
6. I have finished my work. _____ I come tomorrow? No you needn't.
7. _____ God bless you with good health!
8. After the fright that he got I _____ say that he will never go near that place again.
9. You _____ not worry. He is out of danger now.
10. Rilly _____ consult the astrologer on all matters.

## Activity : (might, could for possibility in the past.)

1. Work in groups. Read the sad story of Vimlabai and make as many sentences, (negative and positive) as you can to explain the possible reasons.

   a) Why Vimala's marriage did not take place?

b) Why did she go to Copenhagen?
c) Why was she scared badly?
d) Why did she resign?
e) Why did she devote her life to the cause of cows?

**The story :**

Vimlabai was all decked up in her bridal finery. She walked slowly up to the bridegroom. Then to the utter astonishment of all those present there she turned on her heels and walked off! She called off the wedding. A few weeks later she left for Copenhagen. When she returned, her friends were horrified to see her scared face. She acted in a couple of horror movies. I read a snippe in Stardust that said that she had quit acting and was now devoted to the cause of cows.

The teacher can conduct a brain storming session and write on the blackboard possible reason for Vimlabai's actions.

Now, the students can rewrite the story of Vimlabai including possible explanations.

## Making verbs

| Nouns | Verbs |
|---|---|
| admission | admit |
| action | act |
| agreement | agree |
| arrival | arrive |
| birth | bear |
| behaviour | behave |
| certificate | certify |
| contents | contain |
| decision | decide |
| denial | deny |
| death | die |
| envelope | envelop |
| error | err |

| | |
|---|---|
| furniture | furnish |
| grief | grieve |
| health | heal |
| humility | humble |
| imitation | imitate |
| judgement | judge |
| knowledge | know |
| laughter | laugh |
| mixture | mix |
| pretention | pretend |
| pleasure | please |
| possession | possess |
| quotation | quote |
| sight | see |
| tale | tell |
| able | enable |
| beauty | beautify |
| length | lengthen |
| power | empower |
| pure | purify |
| web | weave |
| person | personify |
| service | serve |

## Directions :

Making necessary changes fill in the blanks with appropriate verb forms of :

Pure, dark, sweet, loose, glory, rich, mad, courage, class, vapour, sharp, fright.

1. The water in the dish _____.
2. Chant the name of Krishna and _____ you.

3. The coach _____ the athlete to perform better.
4. Pull the curtains together to _____ the room.
5. Can you _____ these plants under these headings?
6. Heat _____ water.
7. Add more sugar to _____ the pudding.
8. Gosh! I have eaten too much. Let me _____ my belt.
9. Diana's beauty _____ her admirers.
10. Chinmayananda's discourse has _____ my mind.
11. There! Take this sharpner and _____ your pencil.
12. The sudden noise _____ the horse.

## Question Tags

A mini question that is tagged to the end of a sentence is called a Question Tag. When we use Tag question the rule is : A positive sentence has a negative tag and a negative sentence has a positive question tag.

+ with −
− with +

**Example :** Ramanujam is a famous mathematician, **isn't he**?

Diana is not very good looking, **is she**?

The dark words are question tags. In statements which do not contain auxiliary verbs different forms of 'do' are used in the tag.

**Example :** The students enjoyed the excursion, **didn't they**?

You love bittergourd curry, **don't you**?

## Directions :

Fill up the blanks with appropriate question tags.

(isn't, hasn't, can't, wouldn't, won't, haven't, aren't, doesn't, do, will etc.,)

1. You 've travelled all over the globe _____?
2. The film Air Force One was fantastic _____?
3. Narasimha Rao knows 17 languages, _____?

4. You don't drink or smoke, _____?
5. The team has left, _____?
6. You can use a computer, _____?
7. Sharmila Tagore shot some rare birds in Kashmir _____?
8. You haven't heard the latest gossip about Shah Rukh Khan _____?
9. The clock isn't working _____?
10. The terrorists in Kashmir should be sent packing _____?
11. We all enjoy a good joke, _____?
12. This grammar book is really good, _____?

## Adverbs

An adverb is a word that modifies a verb, an adjective or another adverb.

David the 'Chor' creeping stealthily crept up to the II floor and opened it cautiously, swept all the jewels into his bag swiftly, grasped his booty so tightly and was about to get away when the spotlight shone brightly, nipping in the bud his hopes of bearing completely.

'The game is up, mate' the policeman said politely.

Now he is convinced that crime does not pay, certainly.

A number of adverbs end in 'ly', like those at the end of each line in the poem above.

Adverbs usually answer the question how? when? where? how often? and to what extent? — an action takes place.

a) The potatoes simmered slowly in the pan. (slowly modifies the verb simmered and answers the question 'how')
   **Examples :** how :- loudly, brightly, fast, well, politely, rudely.
b) I want you to write the answer immediately.
   (immediately modifies the verb write and tells when)
   when :- soon, today, tomorrow, now, early.

c) He is standing there
(There modifies the verb standing and answers the question where)
Where :- nowhere, here, there, in, out, before, near.

d) He is rather fanatical in his views on religion.
(Rather modifies the adjective fanatical and answers the question to what extent).

To what extent :- quite, extremely, fairly, rather, partly, wholly, completely, much, little, entirely.

Mrs. George is frequently late to work.

frequently modifies late and tells us how often.

How often : always, never, sometimes, daily, often, seldom

The different kinds of adverbs are :

**Adverbs of**

| Manner | Place | Time | Number/frequency |
|---|---|---|---|
| happily | there | already | often |
| strangely | here | afterwards | seldom |
| fast | out | since | never |
| gingerly | in | soon | twice |
| well | down | immediately | firstly |
| **Degree** | **Affirmative/Denial** | | **Interrogative** |
| very | yes not | | when |
| too | by all means | | where |
| quite | no | | how |
| little | not at all | | why |
| almost | not | | |

Relative :
when, why, how, where

1. They lived **happily** ever after. (Manner)
2. Let us go **there**. (Place)
3. It is one o'clock **already**. (Time)

Sura's General English Grammar

4. she lied **twice**. (number)
5. It is **very** hot. (Degree)
6. By all means, be my guest (Affirmative)
7. Why is she looking pale? (Interrogative)
8. Sriperumbudur is the place where Rajiv Gandhi was assassinated. (Place)

## Directions :

**Fill in the blanks with appropriate adverbs choosing from the list :**

ominously, incessantly, grudgingly, voluntarily, simultaneously, inaudibly, good-naturedly, devoutly, diligently, courteously.

a) The accused looked _____ at the judge who had sentenced him to six years imprisonment.
b) The little girl prayed and prostrated _____ in front of Lord Krishna.
c) The weak student worked _____ and managed to score excellent marks.
d) Radhika chattered _____ in class and so was sent to the Vice Principal.
e) Both Ratan and Vikram reached _____ for the gun.
f) When Ram saw Farida trying to fix the tyre, he _____ offered to help her.
g) The passenger cursed the auto driver _____ for exploiting him.
h) While others shirked and hesitated, Vivek offered his services _____.
i) Kunal did not like Rahul, _____ he thanked him.
j) Always treat everyone _____.

## Directions :

Pick out the adverbs and write Time, place, manner, number, extent, interrogative and relative.

**Example :** <u>Time</u>    The lady came to see me yesterday.

1. _____ You left your remote control there, on the bed.
2. _____ I have had hardly any rest since the term started.
3. _____ The British acted cunningly during their rule in India.
4. _____ Has she told you when to meet in Dallas?
5. _____ The task is nearly completed.
6. _____ The bride answered the question hesitatingly.
7. _____ The pilot flew his plane skilfully through the clouds.
8. _____ AB was elected PM unanimously.
9. _____ She was very ill.
10. _____ He sang lustily.

## Note :

The adverb 'fairly' is used in a favourable context while the adverb 'rather' is used in an unfavourable context.

**Example :**
1. Anjana is fairly rich but her sister Kalyani is rather badly off.
2. Priya is fairly good looking but Aktaar is rather plain.

## Placement of Adverbs :

Since adverbs modify verbs, adjectives and other adverbs, the meaning of a sentence depends on the position of the adverb in a sentence.

**Example :** Only Vimal danced with me. (no one except Vimal danced with me)

Vimal danced only with me (Vimal danced with no one else)

The invigilator almost caught a student copying in the exam hall. (Came close to catching him red handed, copying)

The invigilator caught almost 7 students copying in the examination hall. (nearly that number)

1. Adverbs like nearly, hardly, just, only, scarcely should be placed close to the words they modify.
2. When different kinds of adverbs are used they are arranged in the order : (a) Degree or Manner (b) Place (c) Time (d) Reason.

**Example :** Arvind spoke about astrology with confidence (manner) in the auditorium (place) yesterday (Time)

I went to Kutrallam (place) last week (time) for a holiday (reason).

## Note :

Lovely, lonely, likely, silly, friendly are adjectives and should not be confused with adverbs.

# Prepositions

Prepositions are placed before nouns or pronouns to indicate place, source, method or direction. They indicate relationships.

**Example :**   The book is on the desk.

There the preposition 'on' indicates the relative positions of the book and the desk. The forms of the prepositions never change and it is advisable to memorize common ones. More examples : **in** the attic, **through** the stream, **between** them, **beside** him etc.

Here is a list of common prepositions.

| | | |
|---|---|---|
| in | of | concerning |
| up | beside | regarding |
| behind | towards | except |
| near | before | excluding |
| on | since | including |
| under | from | until |
| against | between | unlike |
| past | among | near |
| during | upon | of |
| after | within | off |
| with | without | despite |
| for | beneath | beyond |

## The use of some prepositions :

On is used with days and dates.

At refers to a point of time.

In is used with years or months.

**Examples :** Dev is leaving for Paris **on** Wednesday. I usually have breakfast **at** 8 'o clock. This penguin was born **in** a zoo **in** 1994.

## Into, in

Into denotes movement.

**Example :** He fell headlong into the well.

'In' is static

**Example :** The ball is in the box.

## Beside, besides

Beside means 'next to' or 'outside of'. She was beside herself with anxiety. Come, sit beside me.

**Example :** She ate 2 pizzas besides a couple of hamburgers.

## Between, among

Between is used in the context of 2 persons, places or things. Earth is between the Venus and the Mars.

Among is used for more than two.

Among the many awards that M.S. Subbulakshmi has received, is the Bharat Ratna.

## Since, for

Since 8 o'clock ; since 1980 ; since childhood. For 2 hours, for a time, for years.

Since is used to suggest the point of time at which an action began. For refers to a period of time for which an action has been going on.

**Example :** The child has been running temperature since yesterday.

**Example :** Hemant and Sunita have been married for several years now.

## Directions :

Look at these sentences and fill in the blanks with the appropriate prepositions.

1. You are supposed to be _____ your best behaviour.
2. There is an auto stand _____ my house.
3. The bird flew _____ my head.
4. Amitabh Bachan is head and shoulders _____ the rest.
5. _____ you and me, let this remain a secret.
6. Humpty Dumpty fell _____ the wall.
7. They went for a stroll _____ the seaside.
8. The dog ran _____ the road.
9. Walk _____ St. John's and turn left.
10. The arrow went right _____ his heart.
11. The old man leaned _____ the tree.
12. The tiger lay _____ the table.
13. Who were the gallows erected _____ ?
14. Why, according to Srinivasan would the Martians not be interested _____ or excited _____ Devi's project?
15. What are you looking _____ ?
16. Where did the parrots finally fly _____ ?
17. Reptiles, including the salt - water crocodile and mudskippers are _____ the many wonders of this paradise.

**On :** The milk spilled **on** the floor. I met Ranjani on the train. Ram lives on the third floor. Look at these luscious mangoes on the tree!

**To : from :-** Meena is coming to India for a vacation from Paris.

Many Hindi words are derived from Sanskrit.

**along, across, opposite :**

The sprinter ran along the tree-lined avenue.

I walked along the road from the temple to the bookshop.

The temple is opposite to the bookshop.

## Learn these expressions :

| | |
|---|---|
| Sure of | guilty of |
| depend on | complain of (something) |
| desire for | complain to (somebody) |
| dismissed from | prefer to |
| feed on | agree with (a person) |
| lead to | agree on (same matter) |
| suffering from | agree to (an arrangement) |
| searching for | argue with |
| take after | object to |
| take pity on | famous for |
| in search of | laugh at |
| hope for | laugh with |
| on fire | jealous of |
| by air | injurious to |
| different from | fond of |
| yield to | guard against |
| worthy of | ignorant of |
| trust in | inferior to |
| thankful to | call on (visit) |
| preside over | collide with |
| relieved of | confident of |
| satisfied with | abide by |
| stand by | afraid of |
| part from (somebody) | married to |
| part with (things) | good at |
| write about (something) | on holiday |
| write to (somebody) | on time |
| on the radio | on TV |
| slow down | on the telephone |

speed up
hurry up
break off
break down
give in (yield)
give up (concede defeat)
ring up
at first
in fact
on Sunday
on leave
on the house
(the host will foot the bill)
for sale
beyond help
beneath your dignity

since 1995
compatible with
capable of
largest, tallest, fattest etc., of
glimpse of
switched off
dropped off to sleep
to haunt
no sign of
give to
weigh heavily upon

the birth of
stretched out
thankful for (something)

## Note :

A word can function as a preposition and also as an adverb.

**Example :** Come down

**Down** here is an **adverb** modifying the verb **come**.

He rolled **down** the **slope**.

**Down** here, is a **preposition**, taking the object **slope**.

So, to find out whether a word is functioning as a preposition or an adverb, check whether it takes an object. If it does it is a preposition. If it does not take an object it is an adverb.

**More examples :**

Come along (adverb)

From along the border. (Preposition)

The plane took off. (adverb)

The plane ran off the run way. (Preposition)

# Conjunctions

Conjunctions connect words, phrases and clauses. Conjunctions may be divided into 3 groups as **coordinating conjunctions, correlative conjunctions and subordinating conjunctions.**

| Coordinating Conjunctions | Correlative Conjunctions |
|---|---|
| and | both . . . and |
| but | either . . . or |
| or | neither . . . nor |
| nor | whether . . . or |
| yet | not only . . . but also |
| for | |
| so | |
| still | |
| otherwise | |
| also | |
| nevertheless | |
| as well as | |
| no less than | |

### Subordinating Conjunction

| Time | until | comparison & contrast | Manner & Location |
|---|---|---|---|
| after | whenever | although | how |
| as | as soon as | than | where |
| before | | though | wherever |
| when | | | |
| while | | | |
| till | | | |

| Cause and effect | Relative pronouns acting as subordinating conjunction |
|---|---|
| because | who |
| since | whoever |
| whereas | that |
| why | which |
| so that | what |
| that | whatever |
|  | whichever |

**Possibility**

as if

if

as though

provided (that)

unless

whether

lest

Co-ordinating conjunctions join words, phrases and clauses of equal rank.

**Example :** (compound sentences)

a) She ate **fish** and **chips.** (words joining)

b) **An angry Tom** and **a mischievous Jerry** had a hearty laugh.
(phrase)

c) **Antonio was stupid** but (he) **worked hard** (Clauses)

Subordinate conjunctions introduce subordinate clauses. (Complex sentences)

1. **She swooned when she heard the terrible news**

   She swooned Main Clause, when she heard the terrible news subordinate clause

2. This (**is the house**) Main Clause (**that Govind built**) Subordinate Clause
3. (you) wait Main Clause (till the bell rings) Subordinate Clause.

## Correlative Conjunctions :

They link independent sentences to form longer sentences.

Mahesh not only bought 10 notebooks but also a dozen pencils.

Neither the promises of Laloo nor his threats had an impact on the voters.

## Directions :

Fill in the blanks with suitable conjunctions/prepositions.
1. Kiso lived in Canada _____ ten years.
2. Benhur has been in hospital _____ Monday.
3. Wait here _____ I come back.
4. Two _____ two make four.
5. I couldn't decide _____ to order for Par Bujji _____ Bhel Puri.
6. _____ Vasantha _____ Kannama has come today.
7. Work hard _____ you fail.
8. _____ it stops raining, I shall go out.
9. The man who rang up last evening is Swamiji.
10. He completed the work _____ he had a roaring headache.
11. I shall not go _____ I am invited.

## Interjection

Interjections express strong emotion. They are followed by exclamation points (!) These words or phrases are used more frequently in spoken than in written language.

**Examples :**

1. **Ouch!** you stamped my foot!
2. **Great!** That was really well done.
3. **Wonderful! Marvellous!**
4. Praise be the Lord!
5. Bravo! Encave!
6. Oh! Look out!

Mild emotions are followed by a comma.
Oh, it doesn't matter.

## Sentences

A group of words that makes complete sense is called a sentence. Eg. Her name is Rita.

2. When are you coming home?
3. What a lovely day this is!

Sentences may be classified as declarative, interrogative, imperative and exclamatory. Each sentence contains a subject and a predicate.

## Declarative Sentences :

1. I dislike musky vegetables.
2. The ugly duckling changed into a beautiful swan.
3. Dolly named her parrot Polly.

## Interrogative Sentences :

1. Whom are you going to vote for?

2. Have you done your homework?
3. Are you invited to the party?

## Imperative Sentences :

These sentences end with a full stop but the subject is omitted.

1. Switch off the fan.
2. Wear clean clothes.
3. Drink milk. It's good for your health.

## Exclamatory Sentences :

These sentences end with an exclamation mark.

1. How charming Aishwarya Rai is!
2. What yummy biscuits these are !
3. What a shocking thing to say !

## Subject and Predicate :

We can analyse sentences by dividing them into 2 parts. - the subject and the predicate.

**The subject** of a sentence is a person, thing or a place.

The predicate of a sentence says something about the subject.

Subject – we ; Predicate – Prayed

The subject and the predicate may contain more than one word :

The crying baby disrupted the show

The crying baby: the subject, disrupted the show : predicate.

The predicate contains the verb

The following may function as the subject.

| | Subject | Predicate |
|---|---|---|
| A noun : | Latha | sings |
| A noun (understood) | The faithful | will be rewarded |
| A pronoun | They | are travelling today |

| | | |
|---|---|---|
| An infinitive | To waste time, | is a crime |
| A gerund | Walking | is a good exercise |
| A noun phrase | How to decode this | is a mystery |

## Subject Patterns

**a) Subject + Verb**

| | |
|---|---|
| He | tried |
| They | laughed |

**b) Subject + Verb + Complement**

| | | |
|---|---|---|
| Radha | reviewed | the chemistry book |
| Amitab | is | a great actor |

**c) Subject + Verb + Object**

| | | |
|---|---|---|
| Anu | posted | the letter |
| We | saw | a dinosaur |

**d) Subject + Verb + Indirect Object + Direct Object**

(She made herself a fool).

| | | | |
|---|---|---|---|
| She | made | herself | a fool |
| They | awarded | her | a medal |

**e) Subject  Verb  Object  Complement**

| | | | |
|---|---|---|---|
| Maria | makes | me | laugh |
| The judge | sentenced | the conspirators | to death |

**f) Subject + Verb (V) + Adverbial / Adjunct (A)**

| | | |
|---|---|---|
| 1. She | smiled | brightly |
| 2. She | wept | bitterly |

**g) Subject  Verb  Object  Adverbial/Adjunct (A)**

| | | | |
|---|---|---|---|
| Sonia Gandhi | addressed | the gathering | last week |
| The spirit | possessed | him | in the graveyard |

| h) | Subject | Verb | Complement | Adverbial/Adjunct | |
|---|---|---|---|---|---|
| | Ram | will be | home | soon | |
| i) | Subject | Verb | Indirect Object | Direct Object | Adverbial Adjunct |
| | The teacher | presented | the first rank holder | with a book | yesterday |

## Directions :

Classify these sentences as Declarative, Interrogative, Imperative or Exclamatory.

1. He ran across the road
2. What a liar!
3. She said that she did not know anything about the murder.
4. Please close the door.
5. Always speak the truth.
6. How much does it cost?
7. What a divine temple!
8. Be careful! The Branches breaking!
9. Is this place haunted?
10. What an explosion!
11. I can't hear anything.
12. The noise woke us all up.
13. It was raining heavily when we woke.
14. That's fantastic!
15. Did you like the advertisement?
16. Flush the toilet.
17. Hold hands and cross the road.

## Directions :

**Identify the sentence pattern**

One Example is illustrated : I am happy.

|   | Subject | Verb | Indirect Object | Direct Object | Adverb/ Adjunct |
|---|---------|------|-----------------|---------------|-----------------|
|   | I | am | | | happy |
| 1. | | | | | |
| 2. | | | | | |
| 3. | | | | | |
| 4. | | | | | |
| 5. | | | | | |
| 6. | | | | | |
| 7. | | | | | |
| 8. | | | | | |
| 9. | | | | | |
| 10. | | | | | |

1. They cut the telephone lines.
2. The rocket Prithivi was launched by the Indians.
3. Up the hill trudged Rip Van Winkle
4. The angry dinosaur chased me through the swamp.
5. High tides occur when the moon is full.
6. Sonia Gandhi is a crowd - puller.
7. They littered the beach.

8. You need to take great care when writing long sentences.
9. I took part in a quiz game.
10. During the elections the towns are full of posters.

**Agreement of the verb with the subject Rules.**

a) A verb must agree with its subject in number and person. If the subject is singular the verb must be singular.

**Example :** The bird flies.

The baby cries

When the subject is plural the verb must be plural.

**Example :** Birds fly ; Babies cry.

b) Two or more singular nouns joined by **and** should take a plural verb: Example :- Rajesh, Srinivas and Radha are coming to the party.

c) When two singular nouns are joined by **with** or **as well as** the verb must be singular. When the nouns are joined by **and** it is plural.

1. Govind as well as Ramesh has not gone to the excursion.
2. The teacher with students, has arrived.

d) Two singular nouns referring to the same person should take a singular verb.

Alas! My friend, philosopher and guide is dead.

However, if the nouns are referring to 2 different people the verb should be plural.

**Example :** The philosopher and the guide are dead.

e) When 2 subjects express a single idea they should take a singular verb :

Curd rice and pickle is my favourite dish.

f) The following subjects should take a singular verb :

everybody, somebody, nobody, anyone, someone, anything, everything, something, nothing, each, every, many a, either, neither

Neither of the contestants was able to lift the bow.

Much was made of a trivial incident.

Many a girl has tried to win his affections, but in vain.

Someone is knocking on the door.

When character is lost everything is lost.

g) Subjects joined by **either . . . or, neither . . . nor, not only . . . , but also** — take the verb suitable to the nearest subject.

Either the ID 7 or the LPK is responsible for this disaster.

Not only the teacher but also the students are interested in this project for social welfare.

h) The subject takes the verb that is suitable to it when followed by these words :

In addition to, along with, as well as, with, together with

i) The vulture, as well as all the other birds, is present at the bird meet.

The children, along with their teacher are waiting in the playground.

j) **Several, many, both** and **few** take a plural verb.

Several musicians from all over the country were present.

Many are feared drowned. Both Radha and Shyam have agreed to come.

k) All, more, none, most, some — take a singular or plural verb according to the context.

All are coming to the wedding.

All my work is done.

None of the cake is left.

l) Though collective nouns refer to groups they take singular verbs.

The collection is considered as a whole.

(**e.g.**) The Indian cricket team is the best in the world.

When we want to emphasise the individuals of the team we use a plural verb.

(**e.g.**) The team members are going their separate ways after the match.

m) Some nouns which are plural in form but singular in meaning take singular verb.

(eg) 100 rupees is too much to pay for the excursion.

The news is shocking.

The collective noun number is singular when it has **the** before it and plural when it has **a** before it.

(eg) A number of activists **are** against the death sentence.

The number of people who are against the death sentence **is** very small.

n) Organisations, books, movies take singular verbs even if they end in 's'.

(eg) Johnson and Brothers is doing poorly.

The panchatantra tales is a classic.

o) A quantity regarded as a whole takes a singular verb.

(eg) Three years is a long time to be away from the family.

p) Nouns that appear to have two parts take plural verbs.

(eg) Where are my spectacles?

His trousers are tight.

## Directions :

Select the correct verb

1. Dal and Roti _____ what I usually have for lunch. (is, are)
2. Happy days _____ here again. (is / are)
3. A herd of buffaloes _____ grazing in meadow. (is / are)
4. Herds of buffaloes _____ grazing in the field. (was / were)
5. Each child _____ a picture book. (was / were)
6. Thousands of pilgrims _____ to Vaishnav Devi temple every year. (go / goes)
7. One of the most picturesque places in India _____ Goa. (is, are)
8. Most of my friends _____ in Calcutta. (is, are)

9. These scissors _____ rather blunt. (is, are)
10. A lot of people _____ the serial 'Hindustani'. (watches, watch)
11. The police _____ coming soon. (is, are)
12. Everybody _____ love. (need, needs)
13. 'The Earth's Minerals' _____ very informative. (is, are)
14. The cost of luxury items _____ risen. (has / have)
15. Among the most common diseases _____ conjunctivitis. (is, are)
16. The leaves of the Tulsi plant _____ medicinal properties. (have, has)
17. Praveen and Raj _____ good friends. (is, are)
18. The best part of the trip to hills _____ the scenery. (was, were)
19. The Arabian sea and the Bay of Bengal _____ situated on either side of Peninsular India. (is, are)
20. The country _____ from Kashmir in the north to Kanyakumari in the south. (extend, extends)

## Directions :

**Ask questions beginning with 'why' based on these statements.**

**Example :**

Peter went to the market to buy a fat pig.

**Ans :** Why did Peter go to the market?

1. The rabbit's nose turned pink.
2. Jai Kumar looked up the dictionary to find the meaning of 'Metamorphosis'.
3. He wanted to see a dentist as his gums were bleeding.
4. They left their shoes outside before they entered the temple, as it is a holy place.
5. Little Siddu hid under the bed as he did not want to eat his lunch.
6. She went to the USA to spend a few weeks with her brother.

## Tense

The word 'tense' comes from the Latin word 'tempus', which means time.

## Present Tense

**The Simple Present tense** tells us of actions done always or usually.

Example : The Indus **is** a long river which **rises** in Tibet.

The Ravi, the Beas and the Sutlej **flow** through the Punjab - Haryana plains.

A low watershed **seperates** these plains from the Ganga plains.

The Ganga Plains **form** the largest lowland drained by the Ganga and its tributaries.

Both the Ganga and the Yamuna **originate** in the Himalayas.

The Ganga also **receives** tributaries from the Peninsular plateau.

The Brahmaputra **joins** the Ganga and **flows** through Bangladesh.

1. The simple present tense expresses **habitual actions.**
   I brush my teeth every day.
2. **General truths.**
   Sea water is salty.
3. **For future actions.**
   The Eighth standard students go to the ninth in June.
4. **If type conditional sentences :**
   If you write that letter, you may get into trouble.
5. **For a dramatic effect :**
   a) She walks into the room, sees the headless body and screams.
   d) The singer slips out of captivity, leaps from the balcony and dives into a deep blue pond.

6. In questions and statements containing do, does and did and interrogative sentences.

   **Do** you **know** the truth?

   **Does** he **come**?

   **Did** she **sing**?

   **Am** I wrong? **Is** it time?

7. **In time clauses :**

   When did this **happen**?

   **Adverbs like :** occasionally, generally, sometimes, always, never often etc., are usually used with the Present Tense.

**Fill up the blanks with apt adverbs.**

1. Maharashtra _____ (lead) in the production of yarn and cloth.
2. Textile exports _____ (earn) valuable foreign exchange for our country.
3. A poor monsoon _____ (affect) industries as well as agriculture.
4. Cherrapunji _____ (record) the world's heaviest rainfall.
5. The narrow isthmus of Suez _____ (link) Asia with Africa.
6. Gypsum _____ (be) used in the manufacture of cement and fertilizers.

**The Present Continuous Tense :** is/am/are + $V^{ing}$

It is used for actions in progress at the time of speaking.

**Example :** It is raining.

Generally, these verbs should not be used in the present continuous: know, smell, taste, possess, remember, belong, cost, want, derive, detest, understand, forget, etc.

   I am loving you (Not correct)

   I love you

   I am not understanding (Not correct)

   I don't understand.

The present continuous is also used to express an arrangement for the future.

**Example :** I **am flying** to France this evening. Vicky **is speaking** in the meeting tomorrow.

Adverbs like now, still, at present are used with the Present Continuous Tense.

## Directions :

Write what is happening in the present continuous tense, use these hints.

**Example :**

    I / eat

    I am eating

1. It / rain
2. She / eat / banana
3. My father / read / the newspaper
4. The moon / shine
5. They / chant / mantras
6. The baby / cry.
7. Are you / watch / TV?
8. What / you / go / party?
9. Raman / fly / Tokyo.
10. Are you / feel / okay?

## Present Perfect

I / we / you / they have + past participle. He / She / it has + past participle.

1. This tense is used to express an action that has just been completed.
   eg. She **has gone** into the kitchen.
   **I have exchanged** my Sony TV for Akai.

2. To express an action which began in the past and is still going on
   **eg.** Alayamma **has worked** in St. Peters since 1950.
   This suggests that she is still working there.

3. For negative sentences
   **eg :** She **has not done** it.

4. For Interrogative sentences
   **eg : Have** you **heard** the latest news?
   Yet, just, never, since, already, lately are some adverbs used with a present perfect tense.

## Directions :

**Fill in the blanks with the present perfect :**

1. The plane from Saudi Arabia _____ (land)
2. Pakistan _____ the cricket match against India. (lost)
3. How terrible! I can't go to the excursion. The bus _____ already. (go)
4. Hurry up! The show _____ already _____. (start)
5. Nisha and Rajeswari _____ each other for many years. (know)
6. I _____ to Kishkintha 3 times this year. (be)
7. I _____ the fees yet. (not pay)
8. I _____ Madhuri Dixit. She is beautiful. (see)
9. _____ you _____ the Taj Mahal? (see)
10. _____ you ever _____ pani puri? (eat)
11. I'm afraid you are too late. I _____ already _____ (sell) the washing machine that was advertised in the paper.

## Note :

Phrases like, last month, yesterday, a year ago, in 1997 are not used with the present perfect.

# Present Perfect Continuous
## has / have + been + V$^{-ing}$ + since / for

This tense is used to indicate an activity, started in the past, that is still continuing.

I have been learning Chinese for three years.

## Negative
I have not been lying

## Interrogative
Has it been raining?

## Directions :

**Put the verbs in the brackets in the present perfect continuous tense.**

1. I _____ in Chennai since 1985. (live)
2. Where have you been? I _____ for you for the past ten minutes. (wait)
3. We _____ posters on the wall all the morning. (stick)
4. Shanta _____ for 5B for more than forty five minutes. (wait)
5. She _____ from stomach ache since last evening. (suffer)
6. Ranjani _____ the Veena since last year. (learn)

# Simple Past Tense

The past tense is used to express an action that took place in the past.

**Example :**   India became independent in 1947.

I met Usha yesterday.

## Directions :

**Fill in the blanks with the Simple Past Tense:**

1. The Tiger _____ on the deer. (spring)
2. Mr. Venkatesan _____ two books in his lifetime. (publish)

3. What _____ you do last evening? (do)
4. He was _____ of the crime. (acquit)
5. I _____ to Vitan Supermarket yesterday to buy provisions. (go)
6. The witch _____ on her broomstick. (fly)
7. Nirpuma _____ with fear when she saw the python. (freeze)
8. Shyam _____ a rope to the drowning man. (throw)
9. She _____ some potatoes for dinner. (fry)
10. Govind _____ March Past. (carry)

## The Past Continuous Tense
## was / were + V$^{ing}$

This tense is used to express an action that continued for sometime in the past. Yesterday, last week etc. are the adverbs used with this tense. **Example :** Shiela was washing the clothes when the thief entered the house.

## Directions :

**Put the verbs in the brackets in the past continuous tense.**

1. We _____ for the bus when we saw Deepak. (wait)
2. The maid _____ the floor. (mop)
3. I _____ cococola when the Principal called me. (drink)
4. Reena _____ behind the curtains so she overheard the conversation. (hide)
5. His heart _____ very fast and his eyes were glazed. (beat)

## Past Perfect
## Had + Past Participle

When we talk of two actions performed in the past, we use the past perfect tense to describe the first action and the simple past tense to describe the second action.

**Example :** The spectators left after the match had finished.

After the match had finished — this action happened first. **Had finished** — is past perfect. The spectators left — this is the second action. **Left** — is simple past tense.

## Directions :

Read the following sentences and write 1 for the action which happened first and 2 for the action which happened next.

1. The hunter had fired the shot before Ranjit could stop it.
   a.
   b.

2. I thought the children had drawn the pictures and given them to the art teacher.
   a.
   b.

3. Sharukh Khan was happy as he had got the best actor's award.
   a.
   b.

4. The cement bags had broken his fall so he was uninjured.
   a.
   b.

5. The thief entered the house after the family had left.
   a.
   b.

6. When Diana's driver crashed the car he had just drunk eight glasses of wine.
   a.
   b.

## Directions :

Choose the correct words from the list to complete the sentences. Use the Past Perfect. Eat, Go, Stop, Take, Beat, Reach

1. I was the one who had made the Doklas but by the time I reached home Rajan _____ it completely.
2. Monica beat Graf in tennis. She _____ Graf before.
3. I wanted to ask Vinay to buy some sugar, but by the time I could do so, he _____ to office.
4. It _____ the detective a long time to find out where the formulae was hidden.
5. The train _____ because of a bomb threat.
6. I _____ the stadium before the match started.

## Past Perfect Continuous

This tense is used to express a past action which continued before another past action.

**Example :** I **had been teaching** in Barekpur before I got married.

## Directions :

Choose verbs from the list to complete these sentences. Use the Past Perfect Continuous

search, skate, steal, sculpt, play

1. When I walked in to the house I could see clothes, papers, books and other things strewn about. Obviously, somebody _____ for the secret formula.
2. Peter _____ small amounts of money from the company over a period of two years, but he confessed when he was caught.
3. He _____ non-stop for more than 43 hours ; He won a place in the Limca book of world records.
4. For how long Mr. Azharuddin _____ cricket?
5. I _____ this statue for 6 months and I still hadn't finished it.

## Simple Future Tense

This tense is used to express a future action. tomorrow, tonight, next week / month / year . . . ., soon, shortly, presently, in a few minutes / days / week . . . , in the years to come etc.

are the adverbs of time used with this tense.

**Example :** We shall go to Villupuram tomorrow.

## Directions :

Read these predictions and mark the simple future tense.

## Pisces

The planet of health, wealth and good fortune Jupiter will paint silver linings in whatever little clouds float across your path. Your confidence will rise.

## Aquarius

You will have to alter long term plans but the benefits will be enormous.

## Scorpio

Offer a good deal of warmth it will pay back.

## Gemini

Success will come with less effort than you had imagined.

## Aries

Friends will boost your morale.

# Future Continuous Tense

The Future Continuous Tense is used to talk about something that will be happening at a certain time in the future.

**Examples :** This time tomorrow, I will be going home for the holidays. Next month we will be writing our examinations.

## Directions :

**Fill in the blanks with the future continuous tense.**

1. I _____ a cheese, pizza for dinner. (eat)
2. Perhaps by the year 2000 we _____ trips to the moon. (make)
3. India _____ the world in the near future. (lead)
4. We _____ a washing machine next year. (buy)
5. We _____ our parents golden wedding anniversary very grandly this year. (celebrate)

## The Future Perfect Tense :

This tense is used to express an action that will be completed by some point of time in the future.

**Example :** I shall have stitched the gown tomorrow by this time.

Expressions like next week, by this time, by Wednesday etc are used with this tense.

1. Cheenu Mama _____ Bhilai tomorrow by this time. (reach)
2. By the end of this month I _____ 1 lakh for the Rani Temple. (collect)
3. Siddharth _____ his green toy train by tomorrow. (get)
4. By this time tomorrow we _____ the exam. (write)

## The future Perfect continuous Tense will / shall + have been + $V^{ing}$ + since 1 for

This tense is used when an action is to continue till some point of time or for some period of time in the future.

**Example :** By 8 o'clock the milk will have been boiling on the gas for 3 hours.

## Directions :

**Fill in the blanks with future perfect continuous tense.**

1. The new tutor _____ the students for 6 months now. (teach)

2. The prisoners _____ that pit for 6 hours. (dig)
3. In another 5 minutes Kapil Dev _____ for 10 hours. (bat)
4. Come Wednesday, Bahuguna _____ for two weeks, for the anti-dam cause. (fast)

## Directions :

**Fill in the blanks with the correct forms of the verbs given in brackets.**

1. As usual, work _____ on top of Mr. Ganguli's agenda. (come)
2. There _____ (be) less than 3,000 tigers left in the wild in India and we _____ currently _____ (lose) a tiger a day to poachers.
3. Gone are the days when women _____ the kitchen. (confine)
4. Mariah's life _____ in turmoil for the past one year. (be)
5. I _____ the bridge when I come to it. (cross)
6. _____ you ever _____ a hunch or intuition concerning something you wanted to do? (have)

# Conditional Sentences

## Read this sentences :

If Pandora opens the box, dark furies will be set loose.

This is a conditional sentence for the clause, if Pandora opens the box - lays down the condition for the action expressed in the second clause - dark furies will be let loose.

A conditional sentence has 2 clauses.

1. The main clause and
2. The 'if' clause

Conditional clauses are of 3 types.

1. The likely or probable conditional (1)
2. The unlikely or improbable conditional (2)
3. The impossible conditional (3)

1. This sentence describes an event that is likely to happen. So it is a **probable conditional.**

**Example :**

   1. If the Pisa tower begins to tilt more we'll bring cables to hold it. (possibility)

   2. Do yoga daily if you want to be fit. (advise, command)

   3. If we reach the bus-stand before 4.30 P.M. we may catch the Ladies special. (possibility)

   4. If you have finished the illustrations, you may hand it.

   In the 'if' clause we can use the simple present, present continuous or present perfect tense.

2. **The improbable conditional. Type II**

   1. If I had wings, I would fly.

   2. If I had a million rupees I would give it to you.

These sentences suggest improbable situations. I don't have wings. I don't have a million rupees.

   The sentence pattern is: if clause with simple past verb . . . would, could, might in the main clause.

3. **The impossible conditional** (III)

**Example :**

If you had not forgotten to water the plants they would not have died.

(But you had forgotten so the plants died - so the sentence describes an impossible situation).

Sentences of this type refer to past time.

The sentence pattern is : If + Subject + verb in the past perfect tense, . . . . Subject + would / could / should + have + past participle of the verb + . . . .

## Directions :

**Match the following :**

| | A | B |
|---|---|---|
| 1. | If I had my credit card with me now | I could have finished my corrections in a trice. |
| 2. | If you violate traffic rules | you would have got it. |
| 3. | If the watchman had done his duty | I would have bought that diamond necklace |
| 4. | If I had four arms | the disaster would not have occured. |
| 5. | If you had asked | you will be fined |
| 6. | If you fast on Sivarathri | you'll activate the bomb. |
| 7. | If you press that switch | you'll be benefitted. |
| 8. | If you heat ice | will you let me off? |
| 9. | If I confess | India is an elephant. |
| 10 | If East Asian countries are Tigers | it melts . |

## Active and passive voice :

All transitive verbs have 2 voices.
A sentence is in the Active Voice when the subject is the doer of the action.

Tom chased Jerry (active voice – Subject – Tom)

A sentence is in the passive voice when something is done to the subject.

Jerry was chased by Tom (Passive voice – subject Jerry)

We can transform sentences from the active voice to the passive by turning the direct object into the subject and by using the appropriate form of the verb to be, with the past participle of the principal verb.

We use the passive voice when we do not know who has done the action, or when the doer of the action is not important.

**Example :** He was murdered (by whom)

My house is whitewashed. (obviously, by the painter)

The perfect continuous tenses and the future continuous tense do not take passive form.

Intransitive verbs cannot be expressed in the passive.

## Simple Present (is / am / are + 3rd form)

1. A washing machine washes clothes — Active Voice
   Clothes are washed by a washing machine — Passive Voice
2. Radha loves Krishna — Active Voice
   Krishna is loved by Radha — Passive Voice

## Directions :

**Change the voice :**

1. Dust is sucked up by the vacuum cleaner.
2. Meera waters the roses every day.
3. Gangotri serves excellent food.
4. Everyone knows him.
5. Detroit manufactures cars.
6. Is all your money spent on jewellery?

## Present Continuous
## (is / am / are + being + 3rd form)

| Active | Passive |
|---|---|
| The poachers are killing the tigers. | Tigers are being killed by the poachers. |
| The doctor is giving the patient an insulin shot. | The patient is being given an insulin shot by the doctor. |
| The maid is washing the dishes | The dishes are being washed by the maid. |

### Directions :

**Change the voice :**
1. The mechanic is repairing the fridge.
2. He is poisoning their minds.
3. The tailor is sewing my blouse.
4. He is being reprimanded by his father.
5. Dinner is being served in the blue room.

## Present Perfect
## (has / have + been + 3rd form)

| Active | Passive |
|---|---|
| The chief guest has given away the prizes. | The prizes have been given away by the chief guest. |
| Who has gobbled up my tiffin? | By whom has my tiffin been gobbled up? |
| She has sold her Maruti | Her Maruti has been sold by her. |

Sura's General English Grammar

## Directions :

**Change the voice :**

1. Cinderella has mopped the floor.
2. William has broken the vase
3. She has read this book
4. The letter has been posted by Raja.
5. The cruel man has beaten his dog black and blue.

## Simple Past Tense
## was / were + 3rd form

| Active | Passive |
|---|---|
| The British hanged the protesters. | The protesters were hanged by the British |
| India defeated Pakistan in the cricket match | Pakistan was defeated in the cricket match by India. |
| Raja ate all the chocolates. | All the chocolates were eaten by Raja. |

## Directions :

**Change the voice**

1. William was beaten up by the thief.
2. I am irritated by her rudeness.
3. The cobbler resoled my shoes.
4. The car rally was flagged off by Mrs. Gariyali.
5. She faxed a letter to the P.M.

## Past Continuous Tense
## was / were / + being + 3rd form

| Active | Passive |
| --- | --- |
| The milkman was milking the buffalo | The buffalo was being milked by the milkman |
| She was ringing the bell | The bell was being rung by her |
| They were singing patriotic songs | Patriotic songs were being sung by them. |

## Directions :

**Change the voice :**

1. Dilip was watching the election results keenly.
2. The tourists were littering the picnic spot.
3. The men are binding the books.
4. The promise was being fulfilled by him.
5. She was spinning cloth on the charka.

## Past Perfect Tense
## had + been + 3rd form

| Active | Passive |
| --- | --- |
| Dhanam had swept the room clean | The room had been swept clean by Dhanam. |
| Shanmugam had invited us to the wedding. | We had been invited to the wedding by Shanmugam |
| She had already hung the picture | The picture had already been hung by her. |

**Change the voice :**

1. The priest had opened the temple door.
2. The patient had not been operated on by the surgeon.
3. They had already completed the job.
4. The teacher had made him the monitor of the class.
5. The photographer had promised us a sponge cake.

## Simple Future Tense
## will / shall + be + 3rd form

| Active | Passive |
|---|---|
| I shall present her this book. | This book will be presented to her by me |
| Aunt Kalyani will pay the tuition fees. | The tuition fees will be paid by aunt Kalyani. |
| Ruby will give Zakir a cup of tea. | A cup of tea will be given to Zakir by Ruby. |

**Change the voice :**

1. I shall write murder stories.
2. Will baron Brunfel respond to the challenge?
3. He will do the job.
4. The press will interview the C.M.
5. Will the Bofors papers be made public?

## Future Perfect Tense
## will / shall + have been + 3rd form

| Active | Passive |
| --- | --- |
| The party will have released its manifesto. | The manifesto will have been released. |
| Will he have seen the film? | Will the film have been seen by him? |
| Will the police have arrested the smuggler? | Will the smuggler have been arrested by the police? |

**Change the voice :**

1. The army will have shot down the terrorists.
2. The undertaker will have defeated Hulk Hogan.
3. The farmer will have harvested the paddy.
4. Will the spirits have been exercised?
5. Will the flat have been designed?

## Imperative Sentences
## Let + object be + 3rd form

| Active | Passive |
| --- | --- |
| Shut the window | Let the window be shut. |
| Read the second para aloud | Let the second para be read aloud. |
| Attempt all questions | Let all questions be attempted. |

# Sura's General English Grammar

## Directions :

**Change the voice :**

1. Repair the broken windows.
2. You are requested to meet the principal at 10 o'clock tomorrow.
3. Send him away to a boarding school.
4. Don't spin the ball.
5. Do it at once.

## Change to Passive

1. Here is the recipe for a yummy dish. Mix sweet potatoes, paneer, ginger and mint leaves. Add gram flour and bind to a dough. Take small portions of the dough and put on skewers. Cook in medium hot tandoor till done. Sprinkle chat masala and lime juice on top. Serve with mint chutney.

**Fill in the blanks with the correct voice forms of the verbs given in brackets. Determine the tense from the adverb / adverb phrase used in the sentence.**

1. Arvind _____ his pencil box in the classroom yesterday. (leave)
2. He _____ to church every year. (go)
3. The temple _____ very soon. (construct)
4. I _____ a colour TV with 100 channels recently. (buy)
5. He _____ pooja daily. (perform)
6. Ram _____ here since 1990. (live)
7. She _____ to the hospital as she was ill. (rush)
8. My house _____ next week. (whitewash)
9. The poem _____ by Tagore when he was a teenager. (write)
10. She _____ P.M. if she had got 10 more votes. (elect)
11. An honest man _____ by all. (trust)
12. All the rooms _____ daily. (sweep)

13. Millionaire Shambu _____ last sunday and a ransom of 5 lakhs _____ from his son. (kidnap), (demand)
14. Thami _____ a machine for transforming orange peels into money. (invent)

## Direct and Indirect Speech

When we quote the actual words of a speaker it is called Direct Speech.

**Example :** Sonia said, "I am sorry for the mistake".

Direct speech is set off by speech marks or inverted commas. (". . . . . . . . . . ") It always begins with a capital letter. It is seperated from the reporting verb by a comma.

When we report the substance of what was said without quoting the exact words, it is called Reported or Indirect speech.

**Example :** Sonia said that she was sorry for the mistake.

In Reported speech, we drop the speech marks, exclamation points and the question mark. The punctuation mark must come before inverted commas in Direct speech. In Reported speech no comma is used after the reporting verb. The tense of the reporting verb is never changed. But replaced by apt verbs like told, warned etc.

Reported speech is usually in the Past Tense.

Words denoting nearness are changed into words denoting distance.

## Place & time

| Direct | Indirect |
|---|---|
| here | there |
| this | that |
| today | that day |
| tomorrow | the next day / the following day |
| last night | the previous |

| | |
|---|---|
| evening | night / evening |
| the day before yesterday | two days before |
| now | then |
| these | those |
| tonight | that night |
| yesterday | the previous day / the day before |
| ago | before |
| the day after tomorrow | in two days time |

## Tense Changes

| | |
|---|---|
| is / are / am | was / were |
| was / were | had been |
| had been | no change |
| has / have | had |
| had | no change |
| do | did |
| did | had done |
| had done | no change |
| will / shall | would |
| may / can | might / could |
| must | had to |
| would / should | no change |
| might, could ought to | |

If the reporting verb is in the present or future tense the tense of the reported speech remains unchanged.

**Example :**     **(Direct)** — Pramila **says** "Shila is sick".

                    **(Indirect)** — Pramila **says** that Shila is unwell.

The Principal will say that she **is** happy with our work.

**Universal truths remain unchanged in reported speech.**

**Example :**

The science teacher said, "The earth rotates on its axis." (Direct)
The science teacher said that the earth rotates on its axis. (Indirect)

## Change of Pronouns

| Direct | Indirect |
|--------|----------|
| we | they |
| us | them |
| our | their |
| ours | theirs |
| you | he / she |
| mine | his / hers etc |

## Imperative sentences :

**Reporting Verb :** ordered / requested / commanded / suggested / asked / threatened / warned / advised / told etc. In Imperative sentences the reporting verb is changed to a suitable verb like : commanded, ordered, requested, pleaded, prohibited, forbade etc.

The Imperative is changed into the infinitive (to + present tense)

**Example :**

Direct : Menu's coach to Menu :- "Skip two hundred times without pausing even once".

Indirect :- Menu's coach told her to skip two hundred times without pausing even once.

## Directions :

**Change into Reported Speech :**

1. Officer to the lady :- "Obtain permission to enter the sanctuary".

2. Nisha to the maid :- Sweep under the sofaset.

3. Doctor to me :- "Avoid sweets."

4. Teacher to her students :- "Do not litter this picnic spot and trample the flowers."

5. Latha to her secretary, "Do type this letter for me dear!"
6. Tony to Abdul "Please don't divorce your wife!"
7. Swami Ananda to the people :- "Donate generously for the construction of the Hindu Mission Hospital".
8. The General to his soldiers : "Shoot!"
9. Teacher to Raj :- "Go home."

## Interrogative sentences.

Reporting verb asked / inquired + conjunction − if / whether / question word

1. When reporting questions the question mark is dropped and the statement form is adopted.
2. The conjunction if or whether is used to introduce the reported speech, the question begins with auxiliaries like, is, are, am, was, were, do, does, did, has, have, shall, can or may.
3. No conjunction is used before the question - words who, whom, whose, what, when, where, why, how and which.
4. The word order is inverted.

**Example :**

"Is     she     present?"
verb   subject   adjective

She asked if   she   was   present .
              subject  verb   adjective

## Directions :

**Change to reported speech :**

1. "Do you like snails?" Dennis to his mother.
2. Does Seema like ghost stories? (Seema's uncle)
3. Will you give me a lift to T.Nagar? (hitch - hiker to driver)
4. How much does it cost? (Nalini to the Shop-keeper)
5. Have you read 'Gone with the wind?' (Turakia to Shyam)
6. Are you taking tuition for maths? (Kunal to Govind)

7. Do you know that the longest word in English is Ha? (Vikram to Kisho)
8. What do you think those mosquitoes are talking about?
9. Will you have breakfast with me? (Sanghvi to Vir Praveen)
10. Kasher :- "Anil, did you find the hammer?

## Exclamatory Sentences

**Reporting Verb :-** said / exclaimed / wished

**Conjunction :** that

Interjections are omitted in Reported speech. Phrases like :- with joy, with astonishment, with surprise etc., are used.

**Example :**   (i)    "How satanic of her to say that !"

                     It was satanic of her to say that.

           (ii)    "Thank you"

                     He thanked me.

## Directions :

**Change to reported speech :**

1. What a breath-taking view!
2. May god bless you!
3. Bravo! You played very well indeed!
4. Isn't that kind of him!
5. What a marvellous invention!

## Declarative Sentences :

**Reporting verb :** said / told, **conjunction:** that if told has an object, then told me / her / them / it / us / Rama / Shantha / the audience etc. say/said, if it has no object.

**Example : -** Sushila said, "Reeta, bring your book".

                 Sushila told Reeta to bring her book.

**Directions :**

**Change to Reported Speech:**
1. Suba to Priya :- "Jennifer is as cunning as a fox."
2. He says, " I live in Kashmir."
3. He said to me, " That was a fantastic show you put up."
4. Dad said, "I am leaving for Delhi tomorrow."
5. Meena said, "You promised to give me the recipe for Chowlota Meen"

**Directions :**

**Change to Indirect :**
1. **Reema to Ashok :** "What a tragedy?"
2. **The doctor to the patient :-** "Take 2 pills three times a day".
3. **Minto to Pinto :-** "Have you read, 'A suitable Boy,' by Vikram Seth?"
4. Can you get in touch with me on the Internet? **(Milo to Rama).**
5. "I am going to give you a baby elephant for a birthday present" Sheila to Amrit.
6. "What a crashing bore Babloo is !" **(Vicky)**
7. "Don't write so fast." **(Aktanar to her daughter)**
8: Do not trample the flowers **(watchman to the visitors)**
9. The Master says, "Victory lies at every step and not just at the end of the race."
10. **Uncle Pai :-** "Did you know that the Koel never builds its own nest?"

# Simple Compound and Complex and Compound Complex

To understand simple compound, complex and compound complex sentences it is important to know

    a) What a phrase is
    b) What a clause is

c) What finite and non finite verbs are

d) Co-ordinating and sub-ordinating conjunctions.

A **phrase** is a group of words without a finite verb.

**Example** :

in the garden, seeing the moon, having spoken to her, etc.

A **clause** is a group of words with a finite verb and a subject.

**Example:**

When I was in the garden ; I see the moon ; because Ram spoke to her.

was, see, speak are finite verbs. They are influenced by the subject :
Example : I see, he sees, Ram see, we see

He speaks ; they speak

He was there ; they were there.

A non - finite verb is not influenced by the subject :-

**Example :**

|  | finite | non - finite |
|---|---|---|
| I | am | seeing |
| He | is | seeing |
| She | is | seeing |
| We | are | seeing |
| It | is | seeing |

A compound sentence is made up of 2 or more independent clauses. It is linked by co-ordinating conjunctions like and, but, so, etc.

Vinod was exhausted yet he continued batting.

a) Vinod was exhausted (Main Clause)

b) He continued batting (Main Clause)

**yet** co-ordinating conjunction

These clauses are linked by the co-ordinating conjunction 'and'. These clauses are mini sentences and make complete sense.

### Directions :

Pick out the independent clauses from the sentences given below and underline the co-ordinating conjunction. Refer to the example given :

1. Be quiet and go to sleep or you won't get your presents.
   a)
   b)
   c)
   Co-ordinating conjunction _____

2. She wore a green salwar kameez and went to the party.
   a)
   b)
   _____

3. She was praised by the principal, so she was very happy.
   a)
   b)
   _____

4. Babita covered her note-books with brown paper and sticked the labels.
   a)
   b)
   _____

5. Arun not only has a Toyota but also a Mercedes Benz.
   a)
   b)
   _____

A complex sentence has a main clause and one or more sub-ordinate clauses. The sub-ordinating conjunction introduces the clauses. The sub-ordinate clause depends on the main clause for its complete meaning.

**Example :**
> When I was in the garden I saw a snake.
> I saw a snake — Main clause
> When I was in the garden — Sub-ordinate clause
> When — subordinating conjunction.

**Match these main clauses with the apt subordinate clauses.**

**Main clause**

1. This is the house      as she was sick.
2. It is Shyamla      before I could give her the book.
3. She did not come to work      that Shekar built
4. She walked out in a huff      who told me the good news.
5. This is the rickshaw      because she was surprised.
6. She raised her eyebrows      which I want to sell.

**Simple sentences contain only one finite verb :**

**Example :**
1. The spirit of sacrifice ennobles man.
2. Walking is a good exercise.
3. Hearing the bell, he ran.
4. More people live in villages than in towns and cities, in our country.

## Directions :

Read the following sentences and say whether they are simple, compound or complex. If simple, underline the finite verb. If compound, bracket the independent clauses. If complex, draw 2 lines under the subordinate clause.

**Example :**

**Simple :** She **eats** pongal and vadai for breakfast.
**Compound : He went to the party and (he) had a good time.**
**Complex :** Melwyn told the truth **when his sister slapped him.**

1. He saw a heap of stones on the roadside.

2. Everyone within there fell into a deep sleep just like the princess.
3. Cholera is an acute diarrhoeal disease that is caused by Vibro Cholero.
4. When she was 16 years old she cut her finger upon the spinning wheel.
5. Telepathy is the most common form of the paranormal that is experienced in everyday life.
6. Learn to control and use this success tool.
7. What I want for my birthday is a new music system.
8. It is a mystery to me why people enjoy roller-coaster rides that are high speed and bone rattling.
9. The school where my mother teaches is near the Mandavelli bus terminus.
10. Man is the image of God.

**Transformation of complex sentences into simple sentences.**

1. Change subordinate clause to a phrase. Use an infinite (to + present tense : to talk, to laugh etc)
2. Use a gerund - verb ending in 'ing' functioning as the subject or object of a sentence. **Example : Swimming** is a good exercise.
3. Use possessive adjectives. **Example :** my, our, your, their, its, his, her.
4. Replace subordinate conjunctions. **Example :**

| If | — In the event of, In case of |
| so ... that | — too ... to |
| although | — despite, inspite of, notwithstanding |
| because, since | — owing to, on account of |
| as soon as | — immediately after |

**Examples :**

**Complex :**

1. If you follow my advice you'll win. → In the event of your following my advice, you'll win.
2. I have no books that I can give you. → I have no books to give you.

3. We saw a girl who was very beautiful. → We saw a very beautiful girl.
4. After Ram finished the work he returned home.
   Having finished his work Ram, returned home.

## Directions :

**Change the following complex sentences to simple :**

1. Everyone complains when prices rise.
2. The team which is in red and white, won the game.
3. I picked up the bird that was wounded.
4. Even though I met that man at the cricket match only yesterday, he did not remember me.
5. I bought a sari that was made of silk.

**Change these complex sentences to compound :** Transform the subordinate clause to a main clause and link with a coordinating conjunction.

**Example :**

**Complex :** Although he was painfully shy he managed to give an interesting speech.

**Compound :** He was painfully shy but he managed to give an interesting speech.

1. He was unable to attend school as he was ill.
2. Milk, which is a complete food, should be drunk everyday.
3. The moment the siren sounded, the prisoners leapt to their feet.
4. I came to school on foot, since I missed the bus.
5. He was so drunk that he could not walk straight.

**Change these compound sentences into complex.** (Change one main clause into a subordinate clause. Replace co-ordinating conjunction with a suitable subordinating one.)

**Example :**

**Compound :** Write fast or you will not be able to complete your assignment.

**Complex :** Unless you write fast, you'll not be able to complete your assignment.
1. He is a multimillionaire yet he is very unhappy.
2. He received the fax message and rushed to the police.
3. My voice sounds odd therefore I'll cancel the speech.
4. The bomb did not burst and everyone was surprised.
5. He overslept and missed the train.

**Change from Simple to Complex.** (Expand the phrase into a subordinate clause. Use an apt subordinate conjunction)

**Example :**
**Simple :** In the event of her not coming to the movie, we'll sell the tickets.
**Complex :** If she does not come to the movie we'll sell the tickets.
**Simple :** He is too happy to bear a grudge.
**Complex :** He is so happy that he cannot bear a grudge.
1. On their arrival, we welcomed them with a garland of flowers.
2. Being poverty stricken he could not go to a doctor.
3. Despite being blessed with a divine voice, Lata Mangeshkar is simplicity personified.
4. We heard of his defeat.
5. They stopped the air attack after sunset.

**Change these compound sentences into simple.** (. . . convert the main clause to a phrase. Omit the conjunction)

**Example :**
**Compound :** Brutus is not only honourable but is also trustworthy.
**Simple :** Brutus is an honourable and trustworthy man.
1. She was unable to sleep and so she tossed on the bed.
   (Being unable to
2. She was not a good cook yet he complemented her cooking.
   (Despite

3. In some places Rajesh went over hard stony ground but he never checked his place.
   (In spite of
4. They were after the diamonds and so was he
   (Both
5. You can manage words and make them serve you.
   (By managing

A compound complex sentence contains both subordinating conjunctions and co-ordinating conjunctions. It contains 2 or more principle clauses.

1. **Example :** Ragavan crossed the road and gave the letter to the girl who was standing near the cafe. Ragavan crossed the road: Main Clause; (He) gave the letter to the girl : Main clause ; who was standing near the cafe : Subordinate clause.
2. It is not what we read, but what we remember that makes us learned.
   It is not (Main Clause) what we read (Subordinate Clause) but what we remember (Main clause) that makes us learned (Subordinate Clause).

The non-finites cannot be the predicates of sentences or clauses by themselves.

## Non Finites

**Infinitive**  **Participles**  **Gerund**

Infinitives : to + present tense of the verb.

**Example :** to talk, to laugh, to meditate.

1. Infinitives can function as the **subjects.**
   **To join this course** is to improve your writing.
2. **The object**
   She likes to write horror stories.
3. **Complement**
   I am here to help you.

4. **Verb + infinitive**
   We exercise to be fit.
5. **Adjective + infinitive**
   I am delighted to meet you
6. **too + adjective + infinitive**
   She is too proud to accept the help.
7. **Enough + infinitive.**
   He has earned enough to live happily for ever.
8. Infinitive after question words : **when, how, where, why, who, what** etc. I don't know where to go.

Infinitives are used to replace certain clauses, gerunds and for linking sentences :

**Example :**    Sudhir hopes **that he will get the first prize**
        Sudhir hopes to get the first prize.
        He is **so young that he cannot vote.**
        He is too young to vote.
        Don't forget. Lock the door.
        Don't forget to lock the door.
        **Replace the underlined words with infinitives.**
1. Antony lives so that he may eat.
2. Increasing creativity is important.
3. David does not know sewing.
4. I wonder whom I should contact for getting my P.F money?
5. This movie is so tedious that I cannot sit through it.

## Directions :

**Rewrite beginning with 'It'**

**Example :**    To hike up prices again is unfair.
        It is unfair to hike up prices again.
1. To experience higher states of consciousness, yoga is good.
2. To improve concentration meditate.
3. To be with you is great.

4. To release toxins from our physiology, fasting once a week is advisable.
5. To create world peace banning war is necessary.

## Directions :

**Link these sentences into one using infinitives :**

1. He sent his daughter to Harvard. He wanted her to study business.
2. Diana is very poor. She cannot buy a Morise.
3. She took out the mirror. She wanted to apply lipstick.
4. You are lucky ; you have won the Jackpot.
5. The potato curry is very hot. I cannot eat it.

**Rewrite these sentences using 'too' or 'enough'**

1. The salwar kameez was so tight that I could not wear it.
2. She was very generous. She gave me a thousand rupees for the fund.
3. The candidate was very nervous. He could not speak coherently.
4. The news seems very good. It can't be true.
5. That cookie jar is very high up. I can't reach it.

## Bare Infinitives :

**The root form of the verb without 'to' is called the bare infinitive :**

I saw her **laugh.**

She made me **cry.**

We use the bare infinitive after verbs like : do, does, did (modals), can, could, shall, should, will, would, may, might, must, need and dare.

**Example :**

He dared not disobey her.

It might rain.

Transitive verbs like **watch, notice, see, observe, make, let, bid, feel, hear** etc. take the bare infinitives.

**Example :**

I **heard** her **speak**

He **made** me **do** it.

Phrases beginning with **'had'** and **'would'** take the bare infinitive :

You **had** better **go** immediately.

After **'but'** and **'than'**.

I would rather die than be seen with you.

She did nothing but stare.

## Directions :

**Complete using bare infinitives.**

1. Rahul did everything but _____
2. I would soon quit this job than _____
3. I bade her _____
4. Preethi felt the wave _____
5. We watched him _____

# The Participle

A participle functions as a verb as well as an adjective.

The 3 kinds of participles are :

| Present Participle | Past Participle | Perfect Participle |
|---|---|---|
| Looking | looked | having looked |
| doing | done | having done |
| win | won | having won |

### Read these sentences

1. How to meet the rising prices was his **nagging** worry.
2. I could not put down that **thrilling book.**

In the first sentence the words rising and nagging do the work of an adjective. They tell us more about the nouns prices and worry respectively. Thrilling in sentence 2 tells us more about the noun book.

## Directions :

**Add present participles to these nouns.**

| | |
|---|---|
| _____ | water |
| _____ | girl |
| _____ | country |
| _____ | star |
| _____ | drama |
| _____ | maid |
| _____ | teacher |
| _____ | corpse |
| _____ | labourer |
| _____ | manager |

**Convert these clauses to phrases using the participle construction.**

**Examples :**

| Clause | Phrase |
|---|---|
| A flower that blooms | A blooming flower |
| the woman who was injured | the injured woman |

1. the drain that was stinking
2. the child who was weeping
3. the scale that is broken
4. the secret she had hidden
5. the men who were working
6. the prisoners who had escaped

The Perfect participle can be used to link 2 sentences.

**Example :**

She saw the deer. She ran to pet it.

Having seen the deer she ran to pet it.

They finished building the bridge. They rested.

Having finished building the bridge, they rested.

## Directions :

**Link these sentences using the perfect participle :**

1. The pied piper drowned the rats. He returned to Homelin.
2. She won the prize. She was delighted.
3. We wrote to uncle Pai. We had not heard from him for a long time.
4. The burglar opened the window. He entered the room quietly.
5. The helicopter was ready to take off. The parachutist had taken his seat.

## Directions :

**Link using the Past Participle :**

The gold chain was stolen. The police recovered it.
The police recovered the stolen gold chain.

1. The eggs were broken. They lay under the table.
2. Pirot looked at the glass. It was cracked.
3. The pizza was burnt. They ate it.
4. The tree was blown down by the gate. Janani saw it.
5. Azharuddin was caught by the wicket keeper. He walked back to the pavilion.

# Gerund

The gerund has the same form as the present participle. with **-ing form = talking, swimming** etc. It is used as a verbal noun.

1. Gerund as a subject.
   **Smoking** is injurious to health.
2. Object
   I love **cutting** jokes

3. Complement
   My hobby is **telling lies**.
4. After prepositions
   Vivek was prevented **from voting**.
5. After phrasal verbs
   Sita **put off meeting** her boy friend.
6. After possessives
   Do you mind **my borrowing** your pen?
7. The following words are always followed by gerunds.
   avoid, defer, decay, enjoy, excuse, finish, understand, imagine, keep, forget, mind, excuse him / her etc., it is of no use, it is of no good, I can't help, I can't bear, keep on, see about, leave off, came for, take to etc.,

## Directions :

**Use gerunds in the blanks :**

1. _____ is Raji's favourite game.
2. Vineet loves _____
3. Do keep her from _____
4. Rajesh could not help _____
5. I don't much care for _____
6. His _____ on time was appreciated.
7. I am confident of _____ this round of Anthakshri.
8. She has taken to _____ like a duck to water.
9. I can't bear him _____ such a lie.
10. It is of no use _____ over spilt milk.
11. _____ her stories is impossible.

# Prefixes and Suffixes

The meaning of unfamiliar words can be determined by having an idea of root words.

**Example :**

| Root | Meaning | |
|---|---|---|
| cred | trust | credit, credible |
| tang | touch | tangible |
| tele | distant | telephone, television |
| topos | place | topical |
| tox | poison | toxin |
| scrib | write | scribble |
| vid | see | video |
| urb | city | urban |
| ven | sale | vendor |
| mot | move | motion |

A prefix is a syllable used before a word to form another word.

**Example :** Vision — revision

A suffix is a syllable used after a word to form another word.

**Example :** beauty + ful — beautiful

| Prefix | Meaning | Words |
|---|---|---|
| a | on / in | abroad, away |
| a, an | not, without | anaemia |
| ab | away from | absent |
| ad | to | adhere |
| ambi | both | ambivalent |
| anti | against | antidote |
| auto | self | autograph |
| bi | two | biceps |
| cent | hundred | century |
| co | with | coalition |
| de | down | depress |
| ex | out | exit |
| homo | same | homogeneous |

| | | |
|---|---|---|
| il | not | illiterate |
| in | not | incorrect |
| meta | beyond | metaphysical |
| micro | small | microscopic |
| neo | new | neologism |
| omni | all | omniscient |
| pro | supporting | pronoun |
| quin | five | quintessence |
| retro | back | retractive |
| super | over | supersede |
| trans | across | transatlantic |
| uni | one | unique |
| vice | for | vice principal |
| sub | under | submarine |

| Suffix | Meaning | Words |
|---|---|---|
| able | can be done | lovable |
| ancy | state of | vacancy |
| er, or | person connected with | teacher |
| esque | like | picturesque |
| ette | small | kitchenette |
| hood | condition of | girlhood |
| ian | related to | christian, barbarian |
| ise | make | exercise |
| ism | system doctrine | Hinduism |
| itis | inflammatory disease | bronchitis |
| let | mini | piglet |

| | | |
|---|---|---|
| logy | science of | zoology |
| ship | art/skill | scholarship |
| ous | possessing the qualities of | poisonous |
| arium | place for | aquarium |
| ule | little | molecule, capsule |
| ry | collection of | jewellery |
| ment | action process | development |
| icle | little | particle |

## Directions :

**1. Add a suitable prefix and write the antonym of the words given.**

**Example :** necessary – unnecessary

| | |
|---|---|
| happy | increase |
| common | responsible |
| pleasant | fortunate |
| relevant | appropriate |
| legible | obedient |
| digested | definite |
| possible | moral |
| credible | |

## Directions :

The prefix 'in' means 'not' and 'mis' means 'badly or wrongly'. Read the definitions, add a prefix to the underlined word. Write a new word:

1. Use wrongly _____ use
2. not complete _____ complete
3. lead wrongly _____ lead
4. behave badly _____ behave

2. **Form new words using the prefixes or suffixes given below.**

   1. a, at, ad, anti, astro, physics, normal, sleep, social
   2. un, en, re, ship, age, able, call, workman, marry, expected
   3. omni, auto, ish, de, tele, mobile, child, potent, communication, fuse.
   4. equi, fore, hydro, inter, mine, tell, electric, distant, skirt, national.
   5. uni, trans, sub, bi, semi, lingual, atlantic, precious, form, soil

## Synonyms

No two words in any language have exactly the same meaning.

**Examples :** attractive, beautiful, picturesque, charming – have different connotations. They are all synonyms of the word good - looking.

## Directions :

**Find the synonyms. The first letters are given for guidance.**

1. Aintique, ancient, hoary,  O
2. Response, retort, rejoinder, reply  A
3. Scale, mount, ascend, rise  C
4. Comrade, crany, pal, acquaintance  F
5. Purloin, pilfer, lift, swipe  S
6. March, roam, pace, saunter, amble  W
7. Filthy, soiled, unclean, squalid  D
8. Lessen, reduce, alleviate, abate  D
9. End, extinct, terminate, conclude  F
10. Toll, luzz, tinkle, chime, jingle  R
11. Knowledge, insight, learning  W
12. Freedom, liberty, unfettered  I

## Directions :

**Write one name for these groups :**
**Judaism, Buddhism, Hinduism**

---

diamond, pearl, ruby, emerald

---

volley ball, cricket, football

---

typhoid, aids, plague, malaria

---

India, America, Australia, Spain

## Antonyms

**Antonyms are opposites :**

| | |
|---|---|
| assimilate | disgorge |
| true | false |
| drunk | teetotaller |
| aggressive | timid |
| clumsy | skilful |
| ambiguous | clear |
| mar | beautify |
| curse | blessing |
| fasten | unbind |
| shy | confident |
| smile | frown |
| civil | rude |
| chase | lead |
| fortunate | unfortunate |
| genuine | artificial |
| victory | defeat |
| punish | reward |

sober       drunk
ceiling       floor

## Directions :

**Fill in the blanks with the opposites of the underlined words :**

1. The **fertile** land of Vietnam was rendered _____ by the U.S. soldiers who sprayed it with Agent Orange.
2. A **pessimist** sees only the hole in the doughnut whereas an _____ sees the whole thing.
3. **Pleasure** and _____ generally go hand in hand.
4. To **forgive** is divine. To _____ is human.
5. Never harp on **lack**. Always be aware of _____
6. The students who had **gathered** there were asked to _____
7. If **ignorance** is bliss, what is _____?
8. **Unity** in _____ is the backbone of Indian culture.
9. Never wish anyone _____. Always wish everyone _____.
10. Oh God! Lead me from **darkness** to _____, from **untruth** to _____, from _____ to **immortality**.
11. Glass is **transparent** but cardboard is _____.
12. This material **contracts** when cold but _____ when warm.

## Homophones

There are words that sound alike but are spelt differently and have different meanings.

ale — a drink, Where is the jug of ale?
ail — ill, bother — What ails you, Knight at Arms?
brake — gadget to stop a vehicle. He applied the brakes just in time, he would have gone over the cliff.
break — shatter — Don't break my heart.
bore — uninteresting — What a bore Laloo is!

boar — an animal. Oblix loved to eat wild boar.

peddle — to sell — He peddled his wares.

pedal — That part of the cycle on which you place your foot.
   Depress the pedal and off you go!

principal — main
   Pick out the principal clause from this sentence.

principle — rule
   As a principle, I never meet anyone before breakfast.

stationery — paper, pens, pencils etc. I need a dozen pens.
   Let's go to the stationery shop and buy them.

stationary : not moving. He planted the bomb under the stationary car.

There : Place. Go there.

Their : belonging to them. It is their problem. Let them solve it.

Fate : destiny
   The Titanic was ill-fated. It sank on its maiden voyage.

fete : fun-fair
   They organised a fete to raise money for the disabled children.

## Directions :

**Select the right word :**

1. This shirt is very _____ (lose, loose)
2. Look at that kite _____ ! (sore, soar)
3. Do you _____ what you preach? (practice, practise)
4. Rambo has nerves of _____ (steel, steal)
5. He is as brave as a _____ (line, lion)
6. The new king ascended the _____ (throne, thrown)
7. Ali Baba found the _____ of gold. (hoard, horde)

## Words often confused :

**Centre :** middle point : place the coin in the centre of the circle.

**Middle :** (between 2 points) She parted her hair in the middle.

**Discover :** (find out something that exists) I discovered the letter lying within the pages of my book.

| | |
|---|---|
| **Invent :** | The mixie is a marvellous **invention**. |
| **Doubt :** | (uncertainty) I **doubt** whether Venkatesh will be home by 7 o'clock. |
| **Suspect :** | (have a hunch about someone's guilt) The police **suspect** a militant group to be behind the Coimbatore bomb blasts. |
| **Sink :** | (To go below the surface of water - ships and objects sink) The Titanic **sank** and all the passengers were drowned. |
| **Drown :** | (to die in water - used for people) The Count was thrown into the sea but he did not **drown**. |
| **Vocation :** | (a calling) Teaching is my **vocation**. |
| **Vacation :** | (A holiday) I am longing for the summer **vacation** to begin. |

## Directions :

**Fill in the blanks with the right word :**

1. a) The dwarf fell from the 18th _____ of the building.

    b) What an interesting _____ ! (story, storey)

2. a) His condition has taken a turn for the _____.

    b) Can you make this _____ rhyme? (verse, worse)

3. a) The _____ is fine. Let's go on a picnic!

    b) _____ you come or not, I am determined to go. (whether, weather)

4. a) That's not the _____ way to do it.

    b) Do _____ to me, He performed the last _____ of his mother. (rites, right, write)

5. a) She has been roaming in the hot sun. Now she has a splitting head _____

    b) After the wrestling bout he is in _____ (ache, pain)

## One word Substitutes

That which cannot be heard            inaudible

| | |
|---|---|
| That which cannot be seen | invisible |
| That which cannot be touched | intangible |
| That which cannot be digested | indigestable |
| That which cannot be eaten | inedible |
| That which cannot be believed | incredible |
| Able to express one's feelings and ideas. | articulate |
| That which is compulsory | mandatory |
| Small hollow thing containing medicine | capsule |
| Person who drives a private car | chauffeur |
| Happening or given after death | posthumous |
| Art of handwriting | calligraphy |
| At the same time | simultaneously |
| Easily breakable | brittle |
| A collection of poems | anthology |

**Match the following :**

| | |
|---|---|
| He who boasts | Fanatic |
| He who doublespeaks | Misanthropist |
| He who cooks in hotels | Hosier |
| He who is extreme in his views in religion | Ornithologist |
| He who sells undergarments | Usher |
| He who eats too much | Atheist |
| He who does not believe in God | Glutton |
| He who hates his fellowmen | Chef |
| He who shows people their seats in theatres | Hypocrite |
| He who studies birds | Braggart |

# Similes

A simile is a figure of speech. It is used to compare 2 objects of different kinds having a common factor. Words such as - **like, so, as** – introduce similes.

**Here are some conventional similes :**

As brave as a lion

as cunning as a fox

as stubborn as a mule

as sure-footed as a mountain - goat

as timid as a mouse

as hot as fire

as flat as a pancake

as smooth as velvet

as thin as rake

as quick as a flash

as keen as mustard

as busy as a bee

as black as coal

as blue as the sky

as green as grass

as pale as death

as deaf as a post

as round as a barrel

as bright as sunshine

like 2 peas in a pod

as drunk as a lord

as safe as houses

## Directions :

**Can you match these creatures and their symbolic qualities?**

| | |
|---|---|
| Bull | frugal |
| Ant | deceit |
| Ass | fidelity |
| Bear | innocence |
| Rat | timid |
| Cock | maternal care |
| Dog | senseless chatter |
| Dove | wisdom |
| Hare | insolence |
| Hen | ill-temper |
| Jaybird | stupid |
| Serpent | strength |

## Idioms

In Apple – pie order (very orderly)
to face the music (face the consequence)
to rain cats and dogs — rain heavily
to blow one's own trumpet — to be very boastful
to take forty winks — to have a quick nap
to let the cat out of the bag — to tell something that was a secret
to bite the dust — to be humbled, defeated
to send to Coventry — to boycott someone, refuse to speak to them.
to bury the hatchet — to make peace
a leap in the dark — to do something without much thought
spick and span — very clean
head and shoulders — above everybody
fits and starts — jerky
blaze a trail — lead the way

haul over the coals — punish

to take the bull by the horns — to deal with some matter boldy and quickly.

## Word doubles

Hammer and tongs
touch and go
fair and square
lock and key
fact and fiction
hills and plains
doctor and patient
guest and host
strawberries and cream
tooth and nail
might and main
rough and smooth
high and low
thick and thin
shoes and socks
pen and pencil
skirt and blouse
arms and legs
fingers and toes
cup and saucer
hide and seek
curds and whey
pros and cons
crime and punishment
Alpha and Omega

## Directions :

**Match the following :**

bag, sense, bounds, heart, flesh, rank, substance, odds, bread, now, total

a) _____ and ends
b) _____ and soul
c) _____ and butter
d) _____ or never
e) _____ and blood
f) sum and _____
g) _____ and soul
h) _____ and baggage
i) _____ and nonsense
j) _____ and file

**With an apt idiom from the list given below, make the necessary changes.**

1. Knows which side his bread is buttered
2. always hides his light under a bushel.
3. butter would not melt in his mouth.
4. to play second fiddle
5. carry coals to Newcastle.
6. Cut your coat according to the cloth
7. to go Dutch
8. to cause a flutter
9. to smell a rat
10. Rome was not built in a day.

## Directions :

**Fill in the blanks :**

1. Mohan is a very modest and self-effacing lad; he _____
2. Avinash looks as if _____. He looks harmless and innocent and too good to be true.

3. Vikram is a smart cookie. _____ He knows his own interest.
4. When Rekha was asked to act as the hero's sister, she refused. She did not want _____
5. To take something where it is already superfluous is like _____
6. I advise you to curtail your expenses to the amount of your income. In other words _____
7. Shall we eat out? Okay but I insist on _____. I feel uncomfortable when you end up paying the bill.
8. When Madhuri Dixshit entered the restaurant she _____ _____. Everyone's equanimity was disturbed.
9. I perceive some underhand work or treachery is afoot. In other words _____
10. Worthwhile tasks are not achieved without patience and perseverance. In other words _____.

## Test

Marks : 100
(100 × 1 = 100)

## Directions :

Read the instructions given carefully before you answer the following:

1. Divya's handwriting is **impossible to read.** (Replace the phrase printed in bold with a single word.)
2. I cannot _____ your proposal. (accept/ except)
3. The student **whispered** to the boy sitting next to him during the examination. He was sent to the principal. (use 'for' and replace the word printed in bold by a gerund).
4. We are not going anywhere this summer, _____? (supply a suitable question tag)
5. Nepal is a _____ region. (change 'mountain' into an adjective and fill up the blank)
6. Certain (doubtful, positive, uncertain) (Choose the word nearest in meaning to the word from the list.)

7. Add a prefix and make a new word that means:
    a) greater than man. _____ man
    b) below zero _____ zero
    c) not dependent _____ dependent
    d) wrongly pronounced _____ pronounced
    e) never regular _____ regular
    f) not obedient _____ obedient.

13. Regroup the words to make meaningful sentences :
    a) herd / I / deer / of / a / saw
    b) potatoes / my / likes / sister
    c) Becky / Mrs. Moses / play / to / forbid
    d) away / brown / the / bear / ran
    e) beache / we / fight / the / on / shall

18. Give the opposites of :
    a) odd
    b) freeze
    c) depart
    d) smooth
    e) worthless
    f) recall

24. Complete these proverbs :
    a) Time and Tide _____
    b) All that glitters _____
    c) Pride goes _____
    d) Make hay _____
    e) Opportunity never _____

29. Join the following sentences. Make the necessary changes. Link with : who, which, although, neither, but.
    a) She shouted for help. Nobody came.

b) Tony is not rich. Albert is not rich.

c) The stadium was packed with spectators. They were screaming wildly.

d) This is the painting. It was sold for a million dollars.

e) He stole the jewels. He was not punished.

33. **Match the following :**

    |   | A | B |
    |---|---|---|
    | a) | pros | fast |
    | b) | flesh | seek |
    | c) | hard | Omega |
    | d) | Alpha | blood |
    | e) | to | cons |
    | f) | hide | fro |

39. **Change to comparative and positive degree.**

    a) The blue whale is the largest animal in the world.

    b) Sushmita is the most beautiful of the three.

41. Shah informed me that his relatives had arrived **(change to simple)**

42. **Correct these sentences :**

    a) These news are true.

    b) My grandmother gave me a hundred rupees note for my birthday.

    c) There are 26 alphabets.

    d) It was me who confessed the truth.

    e) Radha wore beautiful jewelleries.

    f) The wages of sin are death

47. **Change to passive**

    a) Someone murdered Billy.

    b) India defeated Pakistan in the World Cup.

49. **Change the underlined verb to its noun form.**

    He <u>achieved</u> wonders. <u>Persevere</u> and you will be successful.

50. **Underline the verbs and state whether it is Simple Present, Present Continuous, Present Perfect.**

    a) Sheshan has often contemplated changing his job.

    b) It rains nearly everyday in October in Cherrapunji.

    c) Do you know that Arundati has written a play?

    d) I am seeing a lot of Arun these days.

54. **Fill in the blanks with 'a/an' or 'the'. If 'the' is not required put an 'X'.**

    a) I saw _____ anasthetised buffalo lying on the ground in the veterinary college.

    b) It is _____ accepted fact that dogs are intelligent.

    c) _____ owl and _____ pussycat went out together.

    d) This is _____ one way street.

    e) The terrorist kidnapped _____ European.

    f) Some animal welfare activists show _____ lack of professionalism and _____ overplay of sentiment.

    g) The price of _____ gold has risen.

    h) _____ greed for money has driven out compassion. He went to _____ prison.

62. **Fill in the blanks with 'is' or 'are'.**

    Mumps _____ contagious.

    These scissors _____ new.

**64. Frame sentences using the underlined uncountable nouns as countables.**

1. Water water everywhere but not a drop to drink.
2. My baggage is packed.
3. I love chocolate.

**67. Arrange the following 50 words into ten groups of 5. Say why each group belongs together.**

1. who, talking, ramble, mule, bunch
2. driving, requested, yours, purple, devoutly.
3. yellow, gaily, bangles, broches, inquired
4. sending, laughing, flock, fox, crawl
5. pleaded, mine, green, wisely, earstuds
6. street, peacock, team, making, his
7. complained, hers, orange, quickly, anklets
8. that, march, where, plod, owl.
9. exclaimed, its, white, cluster, whom
10. which, bee, herd, early, necklace.

**77. Change to plural :**

library, piano, deer, wolf

**81. Complete these idioms**

To cry over spilt_____

Rob Peter to _____ .

A case of the pot calling _____

**84. Fill in the blank with suitable forms of the words given in brackets.**

a) This is the only _____ to this problem. **(solve)**

b) _____ is that period in life when we are carefree. **(child)**

86. **Change into a simple sentence.**

    a) The police did their best but they could not recover the stolen good.

87. She slapped the children. She was rude to her superiors. (link using **'besides'**)

88. I spend a lot of time cooking - I hate it. **(Combine using a gerund)**

89. Give him a bed _____ in. **(supply a suitable infinitive)**

90. A _____ man clutches at straw. **(supply a suitable participle)**

91. **Fill in with apt preposition :**

    a) There is a lot of dust _____ the desk and bookcase.

    b) She is fond _____ music. The students stopped talking _____ seeing the headmistress.

93. **Give the plural of :**

    loaf, fish, louse, genius, formula

98. **Complete by giving a suitable response :**

    My fifth birthday was last year. _____ next year.

99. **Complete by adding suitable past participle.**

    a) _____ anger

    b) _____ improvement